W☀RK SMART BUSINESS

WORK SMART BUSINESS

Lessons Learned from
HYPNOTIZING 250,000 People and
Building a **MILLION-DOLLAR** Brand

By

JASON LINETT

SPEAKER, AUTHOR &
HYPNOTIC SUCCESS COACH

DOWNLOAD
THE AUDIOBOOK FREE!

READ THIS FIRST:

My goal is to make it easier for you to take action, and create your own success.

Just to say thank you for purchasing this book, I'd like to give you the Audiobook 100% FREE!

https://JasonLinett.com/wsbaudio/

MEET JASON LINETT

How can a HYPNOTIST help you grow your business?

Jason Linett has hypnotized more than 250,000 people. He used the principles of rapport and modeling to track what top business performers and professional athletes do differently to build his own million-dollar brand.

As a master of the micro-niche, he speaks to groups around the world and offers hypnotic-success-coaching to share how people in business can put his WORK SMART principles and strategies to use.

"It's going to slow your first year. Most small businesses fail." The worst business advice made Jason Linett an instant success. He developed his WORK SMART strategies and principles to immediately tap into systems for success to rapidly build several six-figure-income businesses. Now, he shares them with you.

Jason is a featured TEDx speaker. He was honored as the "Hypnotist of the Year." He is invited to travel the world sharing the methods that have not only made him successful, but also have been duplicated by others to create their own financial freedom. In addition to coaching private clients, Jason's programs have been downloaded more than a million times worldwide.

Rather than just "hypnotize" you to become more successful, he will help you de-hypnotize the misconceptions, fears, doubts, and ineffective strategies that are holding back your business success.

Don't let the word "hypnosis" scare you. The more successful you become, the more likely you will discover you're already doing this. Perhaps you just call it something else? Whether it's "getting in the zone" or "achieving your peak performance state," Jason will show you how to duplicate your best entrepreneurial and personal success with purpose, focus, and intention.

The process isn't magic, though the results can be magical.

While building a successful business is a great goal to strive toward, Jason is most proud of his ability to do so and be present in the lives of his wife and two children.

Are you looking to create your own personal change or grow your business?

Would you like to bring Jason Linett to your organization or conference as a keynote speaker?

Contact him at (800) 850-7082

Or visit

https://JasonLinett.com/

TABLE OF CONTENTS

WELCOME

You and I are about to begin a fascinating journey.

Our origin stories may be similar. Struck by a jolt of entrepreneurial energy, we were compelled to forge our own path and inspired to start our own business. We both have a burning desire to design our own lives. We've likely read the same books and studied the same marketing gurus.

The quest we're about to take together is going to be different.

From start-up to scale up, I'm going to share my story and give you the easy-to-implement principles of how I've done it. My goal is for you to harness these strategies to create your own incredible outcomes.

I was once the employee living paycheck to paycheck. I spent years climbing the career ladder waiting to be offered my perceived "dream job," and I walked away as soon as the opportunity appeared. I gave up the steady income and guaranteed benefits.

I launched a local business which quickly filled with thousands of individual clients. I routinely raised my rates to balance supply and demand, yet still had to create a waiting list for new customers. I paid off student loans and credit card debt while buying a home for my growing family. I've stood on stages in front of thousands of people sharing an inspiring message. I more than tripled my business from a single six-figure to multiple six-figure incomes. I harnessed the reins of modern technology to reach a global audience and sell hundreds of thousands of dollars of products online.

My story reads like the entrepreneurial dream for someone just starting out. You, like me, probably read similar books and stories of people escaping the nine-to-five lifestyle to go off and do big things.

So why another business book? My story is different. It's not just different because of how and why I've done it. It's different because of what I do.

I'm a hypnotist.

Through influential language patterns and positive motivational strategies, I've helped thousands of clients release bad habits and negative emotional states and to take control of their own lives. Some people would tell you it takes thirty days to make a massive personal change. My clients will tell you otherwise. They've released the enslaving bonds of nicotine and tobacco to rapidly quit smoking. They've closed their eyes on a fear to then reopen them into a world of strength. They've learned the methods to communicate with their unconscious minds to motivate their own success.

The process isn't magic, yet it can be magical. It's a set of skills that anyone with passion and dedication can learn. These methods are widely used in hospitals, by professional athletes, and by top business people around the world.

I've used the principles of rapport and modeling to track what successful business people do differently so I could generate my own success. I ravenously studied it so I could share the methods with others. I've taken this hypnotic way of thinking into the corporate world. The same principles that can help someone instantly let go of a limiting belief are the same methods to consistently scale up a business.

Why "Work Smart?" It's just two words and just two syllables that form an incredible command statement. It's short and to the point. It's intentional. We'll forgive the fact it's grammatically incorrect. Apple told their communities to "Think Different," when any decent proofreader would tell you it should be "think differently." They changed the world. I want you to WORK SMART to change your business and your life now.

Will this book hypnotize you to become more successful? The better question is what misconceptions, fears, or doubts are you ready to let go of? What ineffective strategies are you ready to stop using?

My goal isn't just to hypnotize you to become a success. My goal is for you to become even more empowered as you de-hypnotize the stuff that's been holding you back.

We're going to work with intention. We're going to put motivation and meaning behind what you do. You're going to make it your own. You're going to work smart.

This book is going to give you a road map to success.

This adventure is just beginning.

Hypnotically,
Jason Linett

IT BEGINS

My story opens in an empty office. The floor is littered with unpacked cardboard boxes. The space desperately needs cleaning. This was it. I had launched my business. I signed a big, scary lease, and I did not have a safety net. I was truly "all in" as I had prepaid the entire year's rent with one check.

I had no other option but to succeed. I gave myself no other options. There was no "out" as I had a growing family at home and bills to be paid. My efforts needed to be direct, intentional, and effective. I had to WORK SMART.

I was doing something brand new and outside the ordinary. I kept running into the issue that I didn't fit into a simple box on a checklist. What category should the business license be? How do I explain my profession to get approved for a business checking account?

I had to figure it out on my own by trial and error, and I had to be prepared for every professional interaction to include the sentence, "No really, I'm a hypnotist." The situation seemed to be stacked against me.

Now, a decade later, I wouldn't have wanted it any other way. In the upcoming chapter "Build Assets and Leverage Them," you'll learn the methods to hypnotically shift your thinking from a "problem" mindset into a "solution" mindset in a matter of seconds.

The empty-office-challenge drove me to be tenacious and "level up" my business game every year. Stand by for some exciting lessons to be learned from an awkward childhood learning magic tricks, playing video games, and then getting into weightlifting. The most inspiring stories may come from rather unique experiences.

I meet too many people who are right at the edge of something incredible. Just one step in a new direction, and you could change your life for good. Unfortunately, people are stuck in analysis paralysis. They've become experts at planning for their success rather than creating their success. They're fooling themselves into thinking they're being productive while, unfortunately, not moving their business forward. There's an expectation of a magical method; that one little thing they need to do that will create all the results they've dreamed of. Instead of really focusing on their best strategies, they place the blame on the methods. They end up with half-baked ideas that never come to be.

People blame the methods they're using for their lack of success. Print advertising is dead. Social media ads no longer work. People don't like to speak on the phone anymore. Whatever the reasons they present, it's not the methods themselves that are flawed, it is the strategy they applied to these platforms.

It's very rarely the platform, it's almost always the strategy.

To WORK SMART is to take a step back and ask yourself, "How can I make this thing work even better?" The solution is to take action. Harness a tenacious spirit, and step into an inspiring mindset of certainty and success. When you change your thinking, you change your focus. When you change your focus, you change your results.

It's time to empower a revolution of business owners who take control of their own minds. Yes, this book will teach you how to do self-hypnosis, and it will also teach you to BE HYPNOTIC. Hypnosis is a process. To BE HYPNOTIC is a lifestyle. The problem isn't the platform of what they're using to grow their business. The issue is the "how" and "why" of their strategy in attempting to make it happen.

I started my business standing in an empty office without furniture and massively in debt. I've now built several six-figure businesses. I've helped to pioneer how education is spread. I've been invited to speak internationally at various conventions and associations.

I was awarded by my peers as the "Hypnotist of the Year." I was invited to do a TEDx talk. I've coached thousands of others to harness the momentum of their own lives to build thriving businesses.

It's not just about work and making money. There must be a balance. I've built these businesses while enjoying time with a growing family, taking vacations, regular date nights out with my wife, and being at home in the evening to have dinner with my family.

This book is about you. What are your goals? What entrepreneurial idea of yours is bursting at the seams? What business opportunity do you keep thinking about?

Imagine shifting your life in the direction you want as you enjoy your adventure toward greater success. Getting there can be just as fun as the results you will create.

My goal is to help you WORK SMART. That doesn't mean it will all be easy. Some of it will take serious effort and challenge what seems safe. I believe there's a myth of safety in having a "steady job," as I've met many people who firmly believed their best option was to keep working for someone else because "employment equals safety." They held onto the belief that they couldn't provide for themselves without the benefits their employer provided them.

I have discovered a much stronger safety net by taking responsibility for my own career and entrepreneurial journey. When you learn to command your own success, you build your own security.

I promise this book will train you to train your brain to WORK SMART. Take old ideas that previously didn't work and find that mechanism to make it work even better. Hypnotically shift your perspective to rapidly reframe a scenario out of a challenge and into a solution. Rethink your business as a network of relationships, and you'll always know where you are. Discover the limitless opportunities in the world around you to easily scale up your success year-after-year.

For the entrepreneur, this is your opportunity to take an idea and convert it into a continuous income stream.

If you enjoy your career as an employee, you will learn methods to position yourself as an irreplaceable asset, rather than as a simple commodity. Make this your opportunity to generate greater stability and improve your potential for promotion.

We're just getting started, so let's break down the misconceptions, scarcity thinking, and other doom-and-gloom nonsense that holds people back. The greater risk comes from not taking the chance and wondering what could have been.

This is your time to become an action-taker, rather than an excuse-maker.

Do you know the worst day of the week to start a diet? Someday.

Do you know the worst day of the week to start promoting your business? Someday.

This book will inspire you to put in the efforts, the focus, and the hours necessary to build success and stability. Some of the work may be hard, yet it will be rewarding as you discover how to WORK SMART. Put intention and tenacity behind what you do rather than relying on hope and luck.

"There's got to be a better way!" This classic line from many infomercials has been my subtext for years. This book will show you a better way.

Read this book. Take notes. Follow through with the WORK SMART ACTION STEPS at the end of each chapter. Track your journey so you can review how and why it has worked for you.

My goal isn't for you to become another Jason Linett. There's already one of me. You don't even need to get trained and certified in hypnosis. That's probably not your goal. Follow your passion with the WORK SMART principles and strategies I've discovered and detailed for you. In my field, I'm known as the "hypnosis business guinea pig." I only teach the things

I've done and found to work. And yes, there will be stories of things that crashed, burned, and became expensive learning lessons.

Put this stuff to use. Fold the WORK SMART principles and strategies into your life.

Think about a hammer. You cannot go buy a hammer, save the receipt, and try to return it with the complaint that it doesn't work. It's a hammer. It's a tool, and it will work as well as you put it into use.

You are about to discover ten powerful principles for success and the strategies to make it happen.

Please put them to use.

WORK SMART ACTION STEPS:

☞ You're going to learn that "everything is an asset." The skills, education, and experiences you have are going to craft what makes you unique and why people should do business with you. Grab a sheet of paper and take notes on the skills and abilities you currently have.

☞ To WORK SMART is to have a passion for ongoing improvement. Build an action list of the skills and abilities you'll need to start the entrepreneurial adventure. If you're concerned about technical skills such as website and graphic design, don't worry! There's a chapter in this book which basically becomes a romance novel about outsourcing.

☞ You're going to learn methods to hypnotically shift problems into solutions. Build a list of the things that may be currently holding back your success. For now, just write them down. The action of writing them down is dissociative; it disconnects you from being inside of the problem. You're pulling these conflicts out of the unconscious mind and putting them on paper in front of you. Simply looking at them objectively can often change your perspective.

THE "WORK SMART" MANIFESTO

Intention, purpose, and focus.

Learn from your growth, get back up if you fall down, and create momentum to do it all better.

Embrace the fact that it won't all be easy. Put in the genuine effort to do things that may be difficult, though don't fall prey to the belief that hard work is the only measure of productivity. In our social media world of "no days off" or bragging about the grind of growing a business, too many people are sadly spinning their wheels.

Don't spend the day waiting for the phone to ring or refreshing your email several thousand times.

Harness the networks of social media to build real human connections and share a message with a purpose.

Treat time as your most valuable commodity. You can lose money and earn it back, but time is something you can only spend once.

Do it your way to stand out to the world.

Dig deep into your personal motivation to have a powerful WHY beneath your efforts. What will your efforts give you? What results will you create? What message or legacy do you wish to leave behind?

The darts are more likely to stick if you've clearly defined the target.

Start with the end in mind. What journey are you going to take, and where will it end? Like a game of chess, what pieces and moves will make it happen?

Embrace that where you start is not where you should end up. Growing your business will be a game of ongoing learning, testing, and challenging the model of what's already working.

Become excited when you find something that doesn't work. You will discover the powerful feedback that comes from what others would just label as a failure.

Move forward with confidence, creativity, and flexibility.

Here's a preview of where we're about to go...

THE WORK SMART PRINCIPLES

THE POWER OF PREMISE

Discover the power of thinking differently. Let your mindset become a catalyst for change, an opportunity to observe the world differently.

BUILD ASSETS AND LEVERAGE THEM

Harness your past and current successes. Make use of the resources you already have to level up your business.

PRINT MONEY

There are abundant opportunities all around. Open your eyes to the possibilities to grow your financial freedom.

BUILD RITUALS

Go beyond habit. Lock in your new behaviors as something sacred.

DESIGN SYSTEMS

Discover how you can duplicate yourself. Automate your efforts so your focus can be on growth.

SCALE UP

Think bigger about growth. Build something bigger than you originally imagined as you increase your reach.

HARNESS LEAD GENERATION

Create relationships rather than customers. Position yourself as an authority within your field to provide maximum value... to receive maximum value!

CREATIVE SOLUTIONS TO DISSOLVE PROBLEMS

It's hard to see the forest with all those trees in the way! Rise above challenges with a dash of creativity.

BE HYPNOTIC

Mentally immerse yourself in your desired result. Tap into your unconscious programming to rapidly shift your thinking in ways that pay off big.

KEEP BALANCE

Don't become a slave to your business. Metaphorically embrace the power of making a new entrance to sharpen your business skills.

Every chapter will give you WORK SMART action steps to plot your moves toward greater success. But wait, there's more! We'll also explore the strategies to make it happen.

This book isn't about attraction. It's about action.

Mindset is going to be a big part of this journey. It's mindset put through the filters of research, experience, testing, and neuroscience. Mindset also is about being willing to give yourself an appropriate smack of reality to keep yourself in line. I know I need that sometimes!

Stop saying "That doesn't work." Approach your life from this point forward by asking "How do I make that work better?"

Who else is ready to WORK SMART?

WORK SMART PRINCIPLES

THE POWER OF PREMISE

The worst business advice I ever received made me an instant success.

We're about to explore how quickly you can shift your thinking to observe the world differently from others. When I talk about mindset, it's not just about positive thinking and affirmations. Mindset is your internal game of challenging the myths and misconceptions that stifle success. It's about that smack of reality you can give yourself to rapidly discover new opportunities in your business or even in your personal life. If you operate as if obstacles are a possibility rather than an inevitability, your opportunities for success are greatly enhanced.

You are about to discover "The Power of Premise," a principle in which you choose to shift your mindset in order to fuel your passion. We'll talk about what assets are the most valuable to you in the start-up or scale up phases of your business. You'll learn how to craft a creative narrative that draws in your ideal audience.

Prepare yourself to let every reason why the odds may seem stacked against you become every reason why you're going to make this happen.

It wasn't my original goal to become "the business guy." Instead, a curious series of events decided the specialty for me.

My professional career began in management for performance arts. As a theatrical stage manager, my job was the least creative part of working in professional theater. It was my responsibility to schedule rehearsals, deal with unions, orchestrate the running of a live show, and help all the highly creative people involved get along. Think of this as a higher form of psychological training.

I worked through internships, put in long hours, and "paid my dues" by sitting in dark theaters fine-tuning the precise operation of productions. I rose through the ranks of stagehand to intern to assistant stage manager to eventually joining the union as a stage manager for theatrical stage professionals. My dream job was getting closer and closer, and as soon as it was offered, I walked away from it all.

Just because you're good at something doesn't mean you have to do it for the rest of your life. I don't regret for a minute the experiences I had in this former career. I learned the value of building professional relationships, collaboration within a team of unique individuals, and the importance of precision as sometimes I would have to call a lighting cue on stage based off the sight of an actor raising his eyebrow. Over the course of eight shows a week throughout several months of performances, the precision was always there, that eyebrow raise would always happen, and the lighting change would always occur on time. The moment appeared spontaneous on stage, yet it ran like a well-oiled machine. You'll learn how to "Design Systems" for your business in a later chapter of this book.

The hobby of hypnosis had been growing in the background, so we now rejoin a young Jason Linett standing in an empty office at the start of a new business.

I did not want to reinvent the wheel, so I scheduled time to attend a local networking event specific to my business. I decided to go out and discover what others were doing so I could model their success. My expectations were positive. I was excited to meet others in my industry who would share words of wisdom and encouragement.

Unfortunately, that was not my experience. Though the locals were friendly and welcoming, the message they shared was full of doom-and-gloom.

"It's going to be slow your first year."

"You won't receive any referrals as a new business owner."

"You should have started a part-time business, there's too much risk in going full-time."

I expected to find a room full of people talking about themes of abundance and, perhaps, even the law of attraction. This was far from it!

Fast-forward to the next month. Given the negative reaction from my first meeting, something happened that told me I had to go back. I had a surprise to share. Business was booming. I had a fully-booked schedule of paying clients. The negative tones of "This will be difficult for you," shifted to, "How are you doing that?"

I was back at this event a few months later teaching the group how I had built my business.

Where you focus your attention and what messages you listen to is a choice. There's a lot of negative dialogue out there. The antidote to this negativity is something I call the "Power of Premise." Imagine what will happen when you flip your thinking in a new direction. Rather than immediately accepting negative expectations, train yourself to adopt a flexible mindset.

What if every reason you couldn't do something became every reason you could?

Live by the catchphrase, "I refuse to buy into that premise." It's like the moment of orchestrated frustration in a television infomercial: "There's got to be a better way!"

The story of scarcity beliefs I heard at the networking event did not fit with my business projections. I refused to buy into that premise. Rather than absorb the negativity, I took serious action. If my schedule was open and I wasn't working with a private client, I physically removed myself from my office. I introduced my business at dozens of networking events. I gave as many live talks and presentations in the local community as my schedule would permit. Since I started with no clients, there was a lot of open space in my schedule!

My mission was to represent my work with passion and professionalism. The result? Filling my schedule was easy.

Which do you have more of? Time? Or Money? I meet many people who hold themselves back. They believe they don't have enough money to launch their business. They believe it isn't the right time. Remember, "someday" is the worst day to start a diet. Some people get locked in a position of, "It won't work." Sadly, their dreams fizzle out before they genuinely take action. Remember, "There's got to be a better way!"

Shift your thinking to understand that time is just as valuable as money. In my start-up years, I employed my time as my primary asset. Rather than spend a lot of money, I focused on no-cost to low-cost methods. I preserved my savings and watched my bank account grow.

Go against the grain with the "Power of Premise." I don't want you to think the attendees at this networking meeting were horrible people. The messages and well-meaning advice came from genuine care and concern. I gained an appreciation for these people as their ideas did not come from scarcity or competition. I used it as a catalyst to put in the work necessary to get positive results.

As "time" was my tool of choice, I ventured into several other professional networking organizations. Do you think I was surprised to find the "It's going to be slow your first year" premise was a virus infiltrating many of these communities? I challenged the model, I chose to WORK SMART, and I received very different results.

Sally Hogshead, author of the book *Fascinate, Revised and Updated: How to Make Your Brand Impossible to Resist*, speaks about the idea that "different is better than better." You can be the best at something, yet if nobody knows of you, what good are those skills? There's a history of tech products that were phenomenal, yet they didn't gain commercial success because another product stood out as "different," which made it better. In the world of personal music devices, the Microsoft Zune had features which could have made it superior to Apple's iPod. In addition to your personal mp3 files, you could share your music and listen to the radio on the Zune. However, the iPod stood out in the market as something new and unique. Why were Apple's headphone cables white? Because everyone else's were black.

Being "different" is just one of the ingredients of standing out to your potential audience. You need to be able to "walk the walk" rather than "talk the talk." Your skills need to be effective. Your product needs to actually work. Telling a good story isn't enough to maintain a business. Remember the principle of "10,000 hours" Malcolm Gladwell speaks of in his book *Outliers*, calculating the time necessary to truly become an expert at something.

I'm going to share with you my method to stand out as the authority that you are in your community. An "elevator speech" is a classic strategy in which you craft your marketing message in such a way that in a short elevator ride someone else can understand your business. The classic premise for an elevator speech is to state your name, your occupation, your location, and perhaps a good referral for you. "My name is John, I'm an accountant in Washington DC, and I'm looking to meet real estate agents."

Shift this premise with a strategy I call "The Hollywood Effect." Many movies begin in the middle of the story. The story kicks off with an action sequence. The film now rewinds to the beginning of the story, and you watch the story unfold up to the climactic moment.

Model this storytelling strategy to sweep people into an experience, grab their attention, and become more memorable. Making them care about your message will cause your audience to really listen to you. Use descriptive language to draw in the audience. Kick off with a brief story to establish credibility and value.

"Show" is always a better method than "Tell." It might even serve you to be a little provocative.

"Good morning everybody, today's story ends with murder, so listen carefully. A successful lawyer comes into my office with a major challenge. She's had a lifelong fear of bugs. Her firm assigned her the case-of-a-lifetime. She backed out of it when she saw a cockroach in the courtroom. She's a new mother. She checked into a hotel after her son was born because she saw a centipede crawling through her living room. After our first meeting, she killed a housefly with her bare hand. Who do you know that is ready to release a fear? My name is Jason Linett, I'm a hypnotist, and I'm an expert at helping people release fears."

Create an emotional response to position yourself as an expert in a memorable way. Use the "Power of Premise" to go against the norm, stand out as different, and present your expertise in a way that demonstrates your expertise.

This principle goes beyond business networking. With some creative thinking, you can flip your belief system on an entire industry. I meet too many people who believe their current situation is their only option. A friend of mine was once frustrated at the lack of options he was finding during his job search. He complained, "There are only three companies in this industry I could work with." Something magical happened in a single pause. His frustration turned into a smile and then laughter as he exclaimed, "Well I guess there can now be a fourth!"

The world is full of stories of people launching new products and services. You've likely already read several business books that have now begun to repeat the same stories of tech pioneers who changed the world. A massive change in the world can often be traced to a singular experience.

When you shift your thinking, you shift the world around you. Shift happens.

This is like a muscle in the mind you can begin to grow, and it doesn't matter if you're flexing it now for the first time. I grew up with it. I was raised in a family of entrepreneurs. My parents left their full-time "safe jobs" to then do something unique and out-of-the-ordinary. My mother quit her job as a secretary for a peanut company, and my father left a job driving a truck delivering plastics to launch a successful wedding photography business together.

Create your own opportunities rather than hope they will happen. The actor, comedian, and podcaster Kevin Pollak would say, "If you're not creating, you're waiting." His career achieved an incredible renaissance as he broke away from the mold of character actor and impersonator to become an online media pioneer. He leveraged the experience of having already appeared in hundreds of television shows and movies and took control of his career to create the next phase of his life. He launched the *Kevin Pollak Chat Show*, a podcast and live-streaming-video interview program which has now been downloaded millions of times around the world. The result? His career flourished as new acting roles appeared; he published a book and stepped into the role of director.

It's time for you to stop waiting and, instead, start creating.

What if the power of premise could change your emotional state? Believe it or not, a dash of creative thinking can help you to dissolve fear, stress, and even anxiety.

I grew up a safe and cautious driver. I discovered that if I illegally drove over the speed limit to pass another car, we would end up sitting next to each other waiting at the same stoplight. Why take the risk of getting a speeding ticket? It was easier to just follow the rules. However, I learned the hard way that a local highway is entirely a high-occupancy-restricted road during the afternoon rush hour. Most highways restrict only one or two lanes, right? Nope. The entire Interstate 66 in Virginia is reserved only for those with two or more people in the car.

Imagine my surprise as I'm cruising down Interstate 66 by myself; the sound of a siren interrupts my experience, and the police lights are flashing behind me. At least the officer smiled as he wrote up my traffic offense ticket with a note that read, "driver was in the right lane going the speed limit."

"The Power of Premise" helped me view the experience from a very different perspective. First of all, I learned to not drive on that highway by myself, and I moved through the experience without stress. Yes, I could have just paid off the ticket, but I had never been to traffic court. Sounds like fun, right? I've got the morning off, let's go and see what happens! In the worst-case scenario, I'd have to pay the offense. To be fair, I was guilty. Pending I had the common sense to not say offensive things to the judge, I knew I wasn't going to be thrown in jail for driving solo in an HOV lane. I refused to buy into the premise that I needed to be nervous.

Yes, many people were in court that day for much greater offenses. I felt a sense of safety, at least for myself, as the judge explained they reorganized the docket to start with the easy cases and finish with the more challenging ones. "If you've never been here before, stick around for the DUI cases. That's where it gets interesting."

The judge announced the day would start with the first-time HOV offenders. Before I could step up and testify, he asked, "Did you learn your lesson?" I responded, "Yes." The entire experience was over in seconds as he banged the gavel and informed me to "Hit the clerks' office on the way out. Pay the court fees. You're good to go. Don't come back again."

I asked, "Don't you want to hear my story?" The judge smiled and asked me if I really wanted to try my odds. I paid the fees and haven't been back to court since.

Think about it. A potentially nerve-wracking situation was diffused by a dash of logic and the "Power of Premise." I did not buy into the idea that I needed to be nervous. It's like the time I was almost mugged in France. Almost. The truth is, I didn't know we were getting mugged. I didn't speak French, and I didn't notice that this man asking for money was holding a knife. I assumed he was a homeless panhandler and politely said, "No thank you," and kept walking. As we moved out of this dark alley, my wife exclaimed, "He had a knife!" Ignorance is bliss when you're too naive to realize someone is sticking you up for money with a knife.

As I speak to organizations about strategies for better innovation and achieving their goals, I've discovered corporations and associations are also in need of the

"Power of Premise." I'm often invited to give a keynote presentation to help reinforce the future growth of their industry. In spite of this positive future goal, businesses are often retreating by toning down spending or reducing their efforts. They're waving the white flag rather than embracing a challenge. The more successful the company I speak to, the more likely they're doubling down their efforts to inspire the right message to their team.

The "Power of Premise" can flip the negative news cycle of a down economy into limitless potential for growth. "How can I make this work even better?" Break out of the analysis paralysis myth that perhaps the timing isn't right and, instead, WORK SMART to make it the right time.

Remember those old movies with Judy Garland and Mickey Rooney? (Please note that my cultural references will gradually become more outdated and oddly specific.) For some reason, they kept finding the need to put on a performance. These movies became formulaic. The solution to all their problems was for someone to say, "My uncle has a barn, let's put on a show!"

It's like standing in an empty office, in debt, and deciding this is the perfect positioning to launch a business. It's like being an entrepreneur with a wife, two children, a dog, and a cat. "I'm going to make this work." Sounds like a powerful premise to live by, doesn't it?

A married couple often debates for years if it's the right time for them to have kids. If they truly have the desire to grow their family, do they wait for the right time, or do they make it the right time?

The "Power of Premise" can help you change your health.

You've likely heard of people using hypnosis for weight loss. It's not necessarily that the power of suggestion can talk to a person's fat cells and directly tell them to die off. Hypnosis can help create the mental shift to motivate the strategies necessary for weight loss. A 1996 study published in the *Journal of Consulting and Clinical Psychology* demonstrated that hypnosis more than doubled the average weight loss of people in an experiment. The people following a diet and using hypnosis as a motivational tool found far greater results than those simply following the diet alone.

I share this research with you as the foundation to tell the story of two different men in their early sixties who called seeking my help in motivating their weight loss. It was synchronicity and coincidence that they had the same backstory and happened to schedule on the same day.

The 10:00 a.m. man walked in and explained, "Now that I'm retired, it's going be so easy to lose weight. I'm going to have time to go to the gym. I'm going to be able to cook and prepare food for myself. This is going to be so easy."

Then came the other man at 12:00 p.m. "Now that I'm retired, it's going to be impossible to lose weight. We're going to all sorts of social environments, we're going on vacations, and I'm going to want to just sit around the house. This is going to be impossible." The first man easily achieved his goal. The second man was struggling to see results until I told him the story of the first guy. The "Power of Premise" was the missing ingredient that made the change possible.

Sometimes there are real conflicts to address. You should factor in the current state of your finances to avoid blindly spending money you don't have. Please avoid sacrificing your personal health and connections to loved ones just to go after a goal. Stay tuned later in this book for "Keep Balance," a chapter devoted to having a life outside of your business. The "Power of Premise" can help you harness genuine conflicts and convert them into advantages or motivational tools.

I once found myself working with an executive who explained that a specific medical condition was every reason why he wasn't successful with one part of his business. His belief systems changed the more we talked about it. As he now put it, "Because I've got this disability, it's every reason I owe it to myself and my community to become massively successful." The premise of his life shifted out of the stuck issue of being a victim and, instead, into the role of survivor and advocate.

Put the "Power of Premise" to use right away. The formula is simple. Take every reason you believe you can't and let it become every reason you can. The word "because" could be the most dangerous word you use. It could also be the most inspiring. Let your current situation be the "because" you're going to WORK SMART in your business. Move beyond "I could" to inspire the mindset "I will."

Once again, "There's got to be a better way."

WORK SMART ACTION STEPS:

☞ You can have reasons, or you can have results. Compile a list of the "reasons" you may have been persuading yourself as to why you can't achieve a certain outcome. Let your creative mind have some fun considering all the alternatives in which these potential conflicts can become your best motivators. Let yourself truly discover that the logic works in both directions, and let the better mindset take hold.

☞ Use "The Power of Premise" to rewrite your personal origin story. Like a superhero, take the elements that demonstrate your readiness to move forward in your new business adventure. This is the story you will now tell yourself to stay motivated and continue to grow. Maintain the truth and integrity of what happened, though realize you can shine a metaphorical spotlight to position yourself as the hero in the next part of your story.

☞ Mark Twain said, "I am an old man and have known a great many troubles, but most of them never happened." Consider upcoming events or possibilities that are causing you stress and exercise your "Power of Premise" to shift your own emotional state.

BUILD ASSETS AND LEVERAGE THEM

I learned one of the best lessons in marketing by watching *The Simpsons*.

You are about to learn to "Build Assets and Leverage Them." This principle will enable you to take physical and mental stock of the tools you have to succeed in your entrepreneurial journey. I'm going to share the methods to rapidly become a peer to your potential customers, rather than to only be looked upon as a vendor.

I will reveal how I turn speaking opportunities into an opportunity to exponentially grow my business. You will get a preview of content marketing: the methods to provide a valuable experience to your future clients, positioning you as the obvious person to work with. You will learn how to listen for client feedback, to harness it, and to turn it into a machine that inspires others to take action.

But wait a minute, there's an episode of *The Simpsons* starting on my television.

"Hi. I'm Troy McClure. You may remember me from such self-help videos as 'Smoke Yourself Thin' and 'Get Some Confidence Stupid.'"

The late, great Phil Hartman was the voice of this quirky character. He was a media personality who had a knack of reminding you of where you may have seen him before.

"Hi, I'm Troy McClure. You may remember me from such educational films as 'Two Minus Three Equals Negative Fun' and 'Firecrackers: The Silent Killer.'" The comedic bit extended to the cartoon character's personal life. Once on a second date, he said, "You might remember me from such dates as last night's dinner."

There's actually something brilliant behind this. While the bit was meant to be a parody, I discovered the value of branding at a young age. Use your current resume and personal experiences as a bridge to the next step in a professional relationship. Because I have done X and Y, I can help you with Z. It inspired my communication formula of "make them care before you ask them to listen."

I call it "Build Assets and Leverage Them." If you have a pile of bricks, you can build a house. If you have money in savings, you can invest it.

Assets are not just physical objects. They can be skills, knowledge, testimonials, or stories. Take the experiences you already have and domino them into the next step of your entrepreneurial journey. What can you do with your previous experience? Who needs to know these assets exist?

The formula I'm sharing here to "Build Assets and Leverage Them" is the foundation of a later chapter called "Scale Up." To scale your business is to let it grow exponentially. I would encourage you to install the question in your mind: "Will this give me more of the same, or will it help me scale up?" The goal of growth is to scale up. We're now going to harness your physical and metaphorical assets to make it happen.

Have you ever had the opportunity to appear at some kind of vendor fair? Whether you have a product or a service, there's often an event where people stand behind tables and talk about their business, and it's as if the attendees walk around to interview the businesses. Their questions relate to "Do I really need this product?" "Is this a service I need?" "Is this better than something I'm already doing?"

I meet a lot of business owners who have done this, and they've experienced frustration. These events often turn into strangers walking around looking for free items to take from your table. This isn't theft, it's common practice for companies to attempt to be memorable by having branded items such as pens, notepads, candies, toys, or whatever, for you to take home a memento of their business. I'm not completely criticizing this. I once gave the keynote at a major convention, and I sent 800 fidget spinner toys home with the attendees.

The problem is that the companies at these events position themselves as a vendor. They're just another person trying to sell you something. The solution? Be the expert, not the vendor.

Take the experience of appearing at this event, the asset, and leverage it into the opportunity for a speaking engagement. I now have an informal rule that I won't appear at a conference and have a vendor room table unless I'm speaking at the event. Otherwise, I'm just a guy trying to sell something. As a speaker, you're in an expert position to demonstrate knowledge rather than be another person handing out branded fidget spinners toys. (No joke, if that's your thing, I know a great source for them.)

The Pied Piper of Hamelin is an old legend where a man played a flute to drive rodents out of town. Spin this metaphor into an effective business strategy as you now "Pied Piper" the attendees from the audience of your presentation back to your vendor table. You've provided value, and this is the opportunity to answer questions, build relationships, and appropriately sell your services.

Stand out in your market by providing value before asking for the sale. When we hit "Lead Generation Marketing," you'll learn more about the astonishing value and methods of content marketing.

Imagine there's a market in which you'd like to grow your business. What if there was a way to demonstrate your credibility in such a way that sets you apart from other businesses? Take note, I'm assuming you have the experience and knowledge to back what I'm about to share with you. Let your actions always have integrity and be truthful. However, if there's a method to demonstrate your authority faster and your work creates raving fans, you owe it to the world to promote what you do.

Here's a story of how I rapidly exploded a segment of my business. I was already doing motivational programs at high schools. I booked these programs through direct-mail advertising, networking, and word-of-mouth. I took the assets of my experience and leveraged it into a strategy to quickly establish myself clearly as a peer within this community. The expert positioning was more effective than just being another vendor sending out a contract and expecting a paycheck.

Market research revealed the name of a magazine that all United States high school principals received. If I called them and asked, "I'm a hypnotist who does a motivational program at schools about making positive choices. Can I write for your magazine?" The likely response would be that they'd send me their current advertising rates. I reached into my toolkit of ethical influence strategies because I knew what I could write for this magazine would serve a genuine benefit for the principals. This method is called a "double bind." Rather than "Can I write for your magazine?" I asked, "Which one of these two topics would most benefit your readers?"

The framework of this question is also making use of what's called an "assumptive close." When will you apply this to your business? That question assumes you're going to put this to use. Would you rather meet on Tuesday morning or Thursday afternoon? That question implies that we are going to meet. Again, if your business truly delivers what it promises, and turns your past clients into raving fans, I would suggest it's your ethical responsibility to use the appropriate methods to motivate action.

I took the asset of my experience and leveraged it into the publishing of an article. The published article immediately served a benefit as the dynamic of my business changed. I wasn't just reaching out to the schools. They were now reaching out to me. But wait, there's more! I took the asset of the article, the marketing lesson I learned from *The Simpsons*, and I leveraged the experience into a direct mail blast to the areas of schools I wished to tour. Attached to a color copy of the article was a customized "Hi, I'm Troy

McClure" style cover letter. "Perhaps you've already read my article? In case you haven't, here's an extra copy for your records. I've already spoken at three of the schools in your county, and I'd be happy to briefly connect by phone to talk about a positive program for your students." The response was incredible. I needed to subcontract programs to other speakers to match the demand.

Model this story. A single phone call leveraged my experiences into an article. I didn't just hope for my phone to ring. I took serious action. Remember Kevin Pollak? "If you're not creating, you're waiting."

The asset will sometimes magically appear. You'll get invited to be on a podcast or radio show. It's not just that you were on the program, it's also who you get to listen to that program. A local newspaper ran a story about my business. I leveraged it by scanning it and putting the image on the homepage of my website. Simply ask yourself, "Who needs to see this?" and the method explains itself.

In my corporate keynote, I teach business people three strategies to internalize goals. One of the methods is self-hypnosis which I demonstrate with volunteers from the group. The majority of my presentations have been for insurance groups, real estate organizations, and large-scale retailers. One day, the gods of Google opened up. I was booked into an industry I've never targeted in my marketing: security and defense. The presentation resulted in an exceptional testimonial from the magazine's editor. I hope you're already guessing what came next! With permission, copies of the endorsement were made, customized "Hi, I'm Troy McClure" letters were mailed out, and I was soon speaking to more companies in that industry.

The stories so far may seem like large-scale efforts, yet they were targeted and specific. Sometimes thinking smaller helps you go big. The article written for the school administrators' magazine was targeting an extremely specific audience: high school principals. The mailing with the defense magazine's editor was only going to one specific audience who would care what that person had to say. The editor was their peer, and I took the asset of his approval of my program to leverage myself as someone who could do the same for other security-based organizations.

You could call these niche markets. I'd call them micro-niche markets. The more specific you get in your business targeting, the more informed you will be to deliver the right message to the right person. As a former member of BNI (Business Networking International), I learned the importance of "Be specific to be terrific."

The more you micro-niche your marketing, the more likely your message will be read and received. I previously mentioned the science of the process and how I've helped people lose weight with hypnosis. Weight loss is a MASSIVE market! It's a billion-dollar industry. Every day there are more people offering a new weight loss system, a new exercise program, or that magic pill that's supposed to fix everything. For what it's worth, the diet pill likely suggests it's most effective when combined with diet and exercise. Want to know how I rapidly lost weight? I dieted and exercised.

Before explaining how I succeeded in offering a weight loss solution to my clients, it may be helpful to know that this concept of "Building Assets and Leveraging Them" is how I made my personal health transformation. I took the unfortunate asset of feeling weak and out-of-breath and leveraged that into the motivation for religiously exercising and eating healthier foods in the right portions. Stick around for "Build Rituals," a chapter in this book which will shift your thinking on how to lock in new habits and behaviors at the speed of thought.

How did I succeed in the weight loss markets? The same method we've been talking about so far: small, targeted efforts to produce large-scale results. The category of weight loss was too vague. Instead, I targeted my efforts on several micro-niche categories. People who were doing a Paleo style of eating. People looking to gain muscle and strength while losing body fat. Realize that in any large community there are many smaller communities waiting for someone to reach out to them.

The best success came from meeting the needs of people living with diabetes who wished to curb their sweet tooth. A man visited my office with this exact goal. Being able to control his sugar intake would help him better manage the condition and reduce his medication through his doctor's guidance. The unwanted habits were easily resolved and, as a bonus, he lost some weight. He happily shared a video testimonial and gave me permission to share it. Through the wonders of online targeted marketing, the video began to roll in front of people who had identified, online, an interest in organizations supporting people living with diabetes. The targeted online market was so small and so specific, yet the response was so big.

His testimonial was the asset. The leveraging came from asking, "Who needs this?"

Assets are things you can create yourself. Are there questions you frequently get asked? Make a video or a special page on your website specific to that question. Is there a checklist you could create that serves a benefit to your customer, yet clearly identifies you as an expert in your field? I was once shopping for car loans and found many of the companies were offering the same rates. Which bank did I do business with? The one that provided a checklist of necessary documents and car-buying-tips for people who are self-employed.

It's time for you to get started. Content marketing is the method of sharing media, such as articles, helpful documents, videos, podcasts, or whatever medium is your preference. In addition to serving as a benefit to the growth of your business, you can reclaim your time by becoming respectfully self-referential in your business. My students can go back and revisit videos from a course. My hypnosis clients get videos and audios reminding them of self-hypnosis techniques. My corporate speaking clients get helpful event planning documents that streamline our working experience. My personal rule for automation is that I'm only allowed to physically remove myself from the running of my business by way of technology if it's improving the customer's experience.

These items can be self-published on your own website. Once created, congratulations! You've got an asset! Ask yourself "Who needs to see this?" Where are the decision-makers that need to discover what you've produced?

Whether it's something you've created or another asset like a testimonial or news appearance, realize that sometimes things take on a life of their own. There's a video of me speaking at a Rotary event that is still floating around the internet from almost ten years ago. That video keeps my phone ringing through organic web traffic. I also direct people to check the link as a mechanism to "meet me before you come to my office."

One of my micro-niche markets are people who already do hypnosis. As much as I have new students coming from the general public who wish to learn more, my classes are often full of people who have already been trained in the work and are seeking refinement to get better results with their clients. I produce a podcast for these people called *Work Smart Hypnosis*. Well that's a familiar title, isn't it? Each recorded session serves as an asset I can then leverage into more people attending my training events.

I must stress that the formula that makes this work is that my #1 goal for the program is to provide a high-value free program for this community. I'm either teaching specific methods or capturing a long-form conversation with leaders in the industry. For a program that's usually an hour in length, less than two minutes of the entire program features a specific promotion. Rather than ask, "What can I sell my audience," my focus is, "What can I give my audience." The side effect is reciprocity. People will find such great benefit from the free resource you share with them that they'll be motivated to want more. Reciprocity is Dr. Robert Cialdini's first principle of persuasion in the classic book *Influence: The Psychology of Persuasion*. Be genuine as you create a valuable asset that you can either purposefully leverage in your business or can use as an organic piece for people to discover you.

You might ask if two minutes of promotion during an hour-long program is enough. A one-hour, prime-time program on network television will feature about fifteen minutes of commercials. This value-first strategy of leveraging assets pays off as my classes are filled, my products sell online, and I'm invited to speak around the world.

I want you to get started. Several action steps are coming your way. Consider testimonials you already have. Do you have special skills? Have you appeared in the news? These are the assets you already own. If you haven't done these things, what can you do to get interviewed, get that feedback, and make these assets appear?

I capture everything. If I'm teaching, the video camera is rolling. If I'm speaking, what other audience should see a video of that talk? If I'm being interviewed, my focus is shared between delivering the information I'm being asked about and considering what bigger audience needs to hear the message? The benefit to the interviewer is that you're helping bring a larger audience to their program.

Leverage testimonials. Leverage success stories. You can even leverage recent news as a reason to consider working with your business. It's also fine to recycle old content. I have videos online that are older than my children that will help pay their way through college.

Assets also empower you to "show" rather than just "tell." Let people see the value you and your business truly represent. Don't just tell them you're good at what you do. As Steve Martin once said, "Be so good they can't ignore you."

WORK SMART ACTION STEPS:

☞ There's a popular marketing term called a "swipe file" where you save images of magazine headlines, emulate direct-mail pieces you receive at home, or match the style of a recent presentation. Don't mimic or copy someone's work, though. Consider their piece a model for inspiration. You could do this. I'd also encourage you to build a master list of your own personal swipe file. Compile your business' testimonials in one place. Make sure you save any articles or media appearances of your business. Make it easy to access these assets in seconds.

☞ Play the game of exploring the micro-niche categories you can target. Do some market research to figure out who are the decision-makers in that industry. Where do these people gather? Review your assets to decide which pieces offer the best leverage to bridge a connection between you and your audience.

☞ "If you're not creating, you're waiting." In addition to compiling your current assets and deciding how you're going to leverage them, get started producing your own content to demonstrate the expertise you clearly have. Show, rather than tell.

PRINT MONEY

Imagine being able to click a few buttons and turn on the ability to instantly earn more money. While this might sound like the false promise of a pop-up ad when browsing the web, you're about to learn how to make this a reality.

From the start, I trust you'll understand that the "Print Money" chapter header is a metaphor. I hope it's obvious to you that I don't endorse counterfeiting money. Instead, you're about to discover a philosophy that realizes that business prospects are abundant. There is no scarcity of opportunity, there's only a scarcity of thinking. You just have to make them happen.

Do you have a credit card bill you want to pay off? Model the stories in this chapter to simply take care of it. Did a tax bill just arrive that you didn't expect? Dissolve the stress and anxiety by running a few business systems to pay it off easily. Is there a silly purchase you've somehow justified to yourself because you just want it? I'm going to share with you the principles to make the money appear to cover the cost.

You're also going to learn the importance of financial responsibility. It's important to only spend the money you have, rather than spending the money you don't have. The arc of business spending I recommend is moving from no-cost to low-cost strategies. The combined efforts of my email automation systems, podcast editors, and web designers are well over $1,000/month these days, but I wasn't spending that when I started the business. My business can now easily handle the expense. Start with what you have and grow from there.

Let's talk about jumping to the front of the line at amusement park rides.

My wife and I love roller coasters. Our kids love theme parks. Living in the Northern Virginia area, the Six Flags America park is less than an hour's drive away. The cost of season passes for the family turns out to be less than visiting the park three or four times a year. It was an easy decision to purchase season passes for the family and visit the park several times a year.

The challenge I'm about to present to you is perhaps the epitome of a "first world problem." Sometimes the best problems in life are the problems we create ourselves. If the conflict I'm about to explain was the biggest issue my family was facing at the time, clearly, things were going all right. I know what you're about to read is ridiculous. This story illustrates that, sometimes, a small investment of money can pay a massive result. Please let this experience inspire much better investments in your life and your business.

Again, my wife and I loved riding roller coasters. However, our children were not yet old enough or tall enough to ride the "big rides." In the mix of watching the theme park shows, riding the family rides together, and visiting the children's play area, she and I would take turns hanging out with the kids or riding a roller coaster by ourselves. The theme park was small enough that it was easy to trade off to ride the bigger rides, and then meet back up with the family. Easy. However, the summer season kicked into full gear, the lines were getting longer, and this strategy wasn't working anymore. Life is rough sometimes, isn't it?

Like most parks, there is an option to upgrade your season's membership with a "skip-the-line" pass. It's not exactly "cutting in line" as the feature allows you to reserve a spot in line without having to stand and wait. You receive a special watch or app to "check-in" for a ride, and the device buzzes when it's your turn to board the ride. It was absolutely a frivolous option that originally seemed completely unnecessary for an extra $200 a year. We wanted to have more family time together at the parks while getting our roller coaster fix. Buying the "Flash Pass" option presented a solution.

Pause the story. I've heard people in the marketing world tell similar tales of buying incredible cars with cash. Purchasing their homes from a single email campaign. Financing their children's college education with a product launch. We're talking roller coasters. I've got sexier stories, yet this one most colorfully illustrates the "Print Money" principle. This chapter could have been about how my wife and I celebrated our tenth wedding anniversary in Italy financed by a single speaking engagement. Instead, we're talking about not having to sweat in line in the summer heat at a theme park ride themed around Superman.

We had the money. It was just a question of whether or not to spend it. Instead, I decided to turn it into a game. I ran an online promotion for one of my programs that typically sells for $600. Through two targeted emails, I added a valuable bonus to open up twelve spots at a special rate of $500. If I was to only sell one unit of the program, the theme park expense was going to be covered for both my wife and I without touching our savings or regular funds.

I didn't sell one. I sold out the dozen within one day, profiting $6,000 thanks to ten minutes of effort crafting an email to offer a special to my audience. The passes were purchased with more than $5,000 remaining for more important life expenses like food, water, and shelter. You know, the important stuff.

This is a strategy I employ on a regular basis. Harness the assets you already have, such as your products or services, and leverage them into quick income. The classic options for a promotion are to either discount, add more value, or, perhaps, blend discount and value together.

It should go without saying that your business strategies must come from a place of honesty and integrity. I insist you only model these principles if you are truly serving your audience and your customers. The people who purchased the program I described above received a step-by-step system to help them better serve their clients and grow their business. Many of the buyers of this specific program have used it to launch their businesses and help hundreds of people on their own. Perhaps you've been on the receiving end of a sale where it was clear the seller viewed you as a potential dollar sign rather than a living, breathing human. Add value to people's lives rather than just taking their money. I urge you to only use your marketing powers for good.

The modern mortgage system makes it a little more challenging for a self-employed person to buy a home. It's absolutely possible, yet that's an industry mostly familiar with tracking someone's payroll stubs from their employer. Just before we were ready to close on our home, the bank informed us they didn't like that we had a balance of a few thousand dollars remaining on a car payment. I ran a promotion similar to the roller coaster story to rapidly erase the debt and move into our home.

Please let this principle inspire you. Had this scenario happened to most people, they would have lost the opportunity to move into their dream home. The best-case scenario for some people would have been that they could have delayed the closing on the property to be more flush with cash, but then they'd run the risk of the sellers getting impatient and putting the house back on the market. Perhaps they'd be able to negotiate to delay the closing of the home to collect a few more paychecks. If they chose to sell the car to rid themselves of the debt, the irony of the situation would be that'd be erasing one debt to take on a bigger debt of the home. The old "rob Peter to pay Paul" story.

Again, I must inject reality into these stories. For those of you in the start-up phases of your business, I'm not going for the boastful story of how I paid off a sports car to buy a mansion. This is the story of paying off a minivan to move into a four-bedroom townhome.

The principle of "Print Money" teaches you to WORK SMART in your business and finances. You hold in your hands the power to instantly change your cashflow.

Buy into the premise that you turn your income on like pushing the button of a printer. When you work from the presupposition that this is the absolute truth, you open your eyes to abundant opportunities for business success in the world around you.

Please resist the temptation to fall into scarcity thinking with several "yeah, but..." objections. Want it to be true, expect it to be true, and you can make it true. The opportunities are abundant; you just have to seize them.

I meet too many people who are stuck in a lifestyle living paycheck to paycheck. I once worked sixty-hours-a-week for a job that only paid me the value of forty-hours' effort. At the end of the year, I was rewarded with less than a 5% raise. This situation is far too common. I vowed never to be stuck in that situation again, and I'll help you avoid it, too.

This doesn't have to be an either/or decision. You don't have to only be the entrepreneur or the employee. You could do both. It's a myth that you must have multiple streams of income. It's a myth that you have to. The reality is you absolutely should.

It's okay to be really successful. I still find it amusing that I have to give this disclaimer when speaking to some business groups. Earning money is not a bad thing. I meet too many people suffering from "savior syndrome," the selfless urge to deeply discount their value or give it away for free.

It's a good thing to earn money. The world is a rather expensive place to live. We have to provide for our family; to have food, water, and shelter. It's important to take the occasional vacation with your family, reinvest in your business, or, as frivolous as it may be, reserve your spot in line for a roller coaster. My clients receive 100% of my focus when we're working together because my attention is on them, rather than a worry if my bills will be paid on time. Remove the "I need the money" mentality from your life. You'll have a stronger ability to respectfully turn away clientele that may not be a fit for your business. There's no need to operate from hunger. Instead, you can lead with service.

My parents are both wedding photographers. I remember the story of a local pastor who published his pricing for officiating a wedding. The man was an incredible speaker and helped couples create a truly memorable wedding ceremony. There was one set of fees if you were a member of his congregation and a rate nearly double that if you were not. There was a brief uproar in the local community as he explained, "My kids should have the same ability to go to college as yours."

As you embrace your right to print money an amazing correlation occurs. The higher the buy-in for someone to make use of your services, the higher the value you receive from the clientele. Keep your ethics focused. I don't endorse charging a ridiculously high fee to give a false sense of perceived value. Charge what your service is worth or, even better, charge what the value of the results will be. Typically, the more someone invests, the more they're ready to make use of what you're going to share with them.

The benefit comes back to you. Reinvest in your skills. Continue your education. Provide a better product or service to your clients. Compete with yourself to improve yourself and your industry year-after-year. The more we're all successful, the more we're all successful. Embrace the mindset that you can print money. There's money out there on the table and, sometimes, you just have to pick it up.

You have assets you have not yet leveraged. There's knowledge or a set of skills you have that others may benefit from. Maybe you know a solution to a common problem. Perhaps you have a better method than how most people do something. How do you discover markets that have not yet been tapped into?

Listen.

So many needs are out there waiting for a solution to be presented. Listen and discover a need you can help satisfy. You have a book waiting to be written, an online course waiting to launch, a workshop others will benefit from, or perhaps a product that will make the world better. Information has value.

Start to think in numbers. What annual income would you like to earn? Divide that down into months, weeks, or even into individual days. Once you have this daily number, reverse-engineer the strategies you need to employ to make that happen. Many years ago, when I wished to double the size of my office, I knew this would also likely double the cost of my rent. By reverse-engineering the income necessary to handle the expense, it became easy to justify the cost.

An editorial calendar can become a game-changer for you. In my business, I know what podcasts I'm publishing and what programs I'm promoting several weeks in advance. This keeps my communication clear and my message focused. It also allows me to balance the art of providing value to my audience more than just making sales offers.

Embrace your ability to print money to experience a shift in your financial strategies. My view of business or personal expenses is now correlated with the income of coaching sessions, keynote presentations, and product sales. The cost of our mortgage or medical insurance for my family may be a financial burden, yet it equates to one day of clients in my office or perhaps the income from one student attending a course. One day of clients or one student completely finances these necessities. Thankfully, I'm in my office more than once a month, and my classes have a nice attendance, so these expenses are less of a burden.

Be warned: don't spend money you haven't yet earned. Unrealized value is money that doesn't yet exist. People talk about the value they hold in their homes, their cars, or even stocks, yet the value doesn't truly exist until someone is willing to purchase them from you.

In the 1990s, Jim Carrey played a character in a sketch on the comedy show *In Living Color*. The bit was poking fun at the popular television psychics at the time. Jim Carrey's character gave an excited testimonial, "My psychic told me I'd win the lottery and quit my job. Today, I quit my job. I'm halfway there!"

Don't spend money you don't yet have, though do embrace earning potential. Even better, make it a game.

I mentioned the goal of increasing the size of my office. Rather than the single room suite, I needed multiple rooms for staff plus a classroom. This move would result in doubling my rent. I installed a mental rule to justify the move: "I have to put on an event every month that, from that single effort, will cover all the expenses of the office space. The admission from just a single day or evening's event should finance the rent, power, and internet expense." My business was already thriving enough to support the higher rent, though I applied the "Print Money" principle to scale up my business year-after-year.

Realize you can "Print Money" to print even more money. In addition to putting on these events, the cameras are rolling. They become my products. One strategy to quantify and qualify a higher expense eventually tripled my annual income.

Let this be a trailer for the upcoming chapter "Design Systems." Every experiment you run in your business is an audition to learn what works best, so you can later duplicate your methods. You can now turn on these machines or "systems" in your business at will. If a random unexpected expense occurs, you will experience less stress knowing exactly how to "Print Money" so you can move on with your life.

Years ago, my websites were briefly shut down because the company hosting my sites got hacked. The code of my sites was breached with viruses and malware, so Google did the appropriate thing and hid my websites from search results. That was appropriate for them. It was horrible for me! Most of my clients were discovering me on the web. If my websites weren't appearing online, this could have shut down my business.

My team began to scrub the websites and migrate them to another host. Meanwhile, I got out into the community, networking and giving presentations on what I do. I ran the "Print Money" principle by falling back on systems I previously found to work. There was no lapse in business. Business only got better as the web issue was resolved.

People buy from people. Create an open line of communication through articles, updating websites, sending out emails, and even posting the occasional selfie video on social media. Provide more value than what you ask in return, so when you do ask for a sale, the reciprocity relationship is already in motion. Give, give, give, give, get.

Let these stories inspire you to take action. Keep an ongoing list in the Notes app of your phone of ideas you are ready to implement. Track your assets and brainstorm how to leverage them.

There's no such thing as finding the time. There's only making the time. Schedule time to design your systems and create the material necessary to supercharge your business.

There's money on the table waiting to be picked up. Yes, you can print it yourself.

WORK SMART ACTION STEPS:

☞ There's no such thing as finding the time. There's only making the time. Schedule time to look at your calendar and plan ahead for timed strategies to print money. Give yourself a specific deadline to create the assets necessary to leverage into income.

☞ Experiment with changing your offers. If you only ever do a promotion themed around a discount, you may accidentally train your audience to wait until you offer a discount before they buy. I won't shop at *Bed Bath & Beyond* unless I have one of those big blue "20% off one item" coupons they mail to my home every month. Test your market by making an offer that comes with the bonus of added value. This could be an additional training, an extra live session, or, perhaps, a personalized coaching call.

☞ Continue your "personal swipe file" action step from the "Create Assets and Leverage Them" chapter. I keep an ongoing list of opportunities in the Notes app on my phone, so these strategies are in the chamber ready to be fired off at the appropriate time. In addition to tracking your assets, track how you're going to put them to use.

BUILD RITUALS

A small shift in thinking can create massive results when it comes to creating new habits. We're about to explore a subtle mindset adjustment to lock in new behaviors at a deeper level of consciousness. Just like a muscle in the body that can grow stronger through consistent effort, you're going to learn to train your brain like a muscle to grow stronger and hold onto new habits.

I'll share with you the personal discoveries I've made to draw lines between my family life and work life. You're going to discover the most valuable asset in your life, and how to best put it to use. Here's a preview: it's not money. I'll share with you how I became a morning person to inspire incredible momentum to jumpstart my day, plus the most valuable lesson we can learn from video games.

I don't want you to focus on creating better habits. I want you to "Build Rituals."

It may be just a reframing of familiar words, yet your mind and body will process your actions differently as you view them as rituals.

Rituals are empowering. Rituals are things we hold sacred. Some people are always in church on a Sunday morning. That's their ritual. Some are always at the bus stop waiting for their kids to come home from school. That's their ritual. Others are glued to the television when a new episode of their favorite show launches. That's a ritual.

I maintain a ritual of waking up early, checking in with my virtual staff around the world, and then hitting the gym early in the morning. The metaphors that come from strength training are inspiring. After physical training, the body enters a recovery phase. After recovery, there's a phase called "supercompensation." That's just an awesome word, isn't it? This is the phase where the body is responding to the training and recovery and is making the judgment that the body needs to adjust to support the effort. Your body compensates in response to the continued effort of lifting heavier things. And that's just super.

Neurological strength increases, and muscles physically grow larger in size, provided the appropriate nutrition is present to support the growth. It doesn't happen overnight. Strength is something that builds over time. Strength is a skill.

While we're on this topic, I developed an embarrassing habit several years ago. It wasn't the typical bad habit. I've never been a smoker, I cut alcohol out of my life a few years ago, and even when I was obese in my teenage years, I didn't have much of a sweet tooth. My bad habit? I kept hurting myself. I would pick up something heavy like a suitcase or piece of furniture with the kind of poor technique that would make a physical therapist cringe. My back muscles would end up twisted and sprained. I'd be in bed in pain for several days.

I visited doctor after doctor trying to discover what was wrong with my back. They couldn't find anything specifically wrong with the muscles, nerves, or bones. What was the real issue? I was weak and clumsy. My first trip to a physical therapist didn't involve the stretching and exercise I expected. Instead, I received training on how to "pick up things like a human." She recommended a few strength training exercises, and I transformed my occasional habit of going to the gym into a five-or-six-times-a-week ritual I've maintained for years. The back pain disappeared as my strength grew.

For anyone looking to gain the insights on how to improve the composition of your body through strength-training, I'd highly recommend the books *Bigger Leaner Stronger* or *Thinner Leaner Stronger* by Michael Matthews. His work was the foundation to take control of my own health.

Model this story, even if physical strength is not your goal of reading this book. I recognized a challenge, found a possible solution, and kept at the new strategy until I got the desired result. Success may not always be an instant result. It's the effort over time that may build an empire. Treat these efforts as if they had the importance of being a ritual, and you'll easily lock them in as part of your life.

To wrap up the connections between building a business and strength, other lessons soon emerged. Strength increases over time. You don't hit personal records every day. Consistency over time and patience will produce the greatest results. Even a runner will only gradually increase their training distance to eventually run a full marathon. Gradually increase the burden so as to not overload yourself too quickly, and endurance will naturally grow. The discipline I've built building my strength has spilled into other parts of my life.

A friend of mine once said, "The way you are here is the way you are everywhere else." Is the back of your car a disaster? Are there piles of papers on your office desk? Are there hundreds of emails you haven't yet responded to? It's likely these are symptoms of larger issues you may be facing in life.

One small change can trigger massive results in other parts of your life. I tripled my business in the time since I got in better physical shape. Decide now to purposefully and consciously shift your life in a new direction. Build effective rituals in your life and treat those behaviors as if they were sacred. This discipline will likely spill into other parts of your life.

Everything comes down to testing. Try out different schedules and behaviors; you'll find the rituals that best align with you. I organize my day now by "modes" to keep on track, harness momentum, and leave the workday easily to be home with my family.

I intentionally operate what I've nicknamed a three-ring-circus business lifestyle. A workweek may include contracts for a speaking engagement, coaching an executive client, or producing training content for my online communities. It would be impossible to balance this without establishing rituals to keep up with it all. This includes when I respond to emails, how I schedule phone calls and interviews, and brainstorm new projects.

I've made it a ritual to schedule time to design new projects, enter new markets, and scale up my business. Be sure there's time to work ON your business, not just IN your business. Thank you to Michael Gerber for his classic book, *The E-Myth Revisited*, a must-read for any business owner. In the upcoming "Scale Up" chapter you'll learn to avoid only working in the patterns of "more of the same." Your business may plateau if you're only doing the same things over and over. Hold yourself accountable to create rituals to go after growth.

There's no such thing as finding the time. There's only making the time. Are there new skills you need to acquire? Is there an advanced title or certification you need in your industry? I've made personal development a ritual. Schedule time for yourself to grow as a person.

Are there communities you need to join? Are there local business organizations you would benefit from by being a member? Lock these times in your calendar as if they're a ritual.

Is your work/life balance suffering? Block off time in your calendar to take your kids to the park, the library, or out for an adventure. Schedule a date night with your loved one or lock off time in advance for a vacation. Let these become rituals that cannot be canceled.

People make it a ritual to attend a live event. You've purchased top-dollar tickets to a concert and, assuming there isn't a major natural disaster, you've locked the event in your life as if it were a ritual. It's different if you were just thinking of seeing a movie in the theater. If, suddenly, the weather turned and it started to rain, you might decide to wait a few months to stream the movie at home, instead.

Rituals can also be small things. The time you brush your teeth each day is a ritual. So is where you charge your mobile phone. If you can do these things consistently, realize how easy it's going to be to create other rituals that will improve your quality of life.

Take a moment to think big. Let's go after some massive goals here. Do you want to write a book? Are you ready to launch an online training program? Is there a renovation project at home you'd like to finance? Is there a major health goal you'd like to achieve? Start with the end in mind, and reverse-engineer the rituals necessary to make it happen.

Speaking of money, there's familiar advice for someone in their first paying job. It's recommended they start saving for their future, perhaps with a savings account or retirement savings program. This is often called "pay yourself first." Take a small percentage of your income and automatically set it aside. We'll always have liabilities, bills, and taxes, and we'll always have to pay for food, water, and power.

If you make it a priority to pay yourself first you often still make ends meet. Live as if that 10% of your income wasn't yours to spend. We make unconscious adjustments to create balance. Maybe you wait for the movie to stream online rather than drop twenty dollars to see it in the theater, especially with that rainstorm I previously mentioned. Perhaps you make your coffee from home rather than give the coffee shop six dollars for a cup. You might pack your lunch some days rather than give the restaurant near your work eighteen dollars for a salad.

By setting the money aside, you're vowing to live as if that money wasn't yours to spend. Pay yourself first. It will produce huge dividends in your future. Pennies invested now could become thousands of dollars over time.

Financial strategy is a part of the WORK SMART mindset. Just realize the most valuable asset you have isn't money. It's time. Time is something that if you don't spend it wisely, you don't get to enjoy it in the future. Pay yourself first with your own time. Make this a ritual as early as today. Make time for yourself, your family, and your business.

To WORK SMART is to work with intention, purpose, and focus. Embrace the philosophy that there is no failure, there's only feedback. Harness the learning that you receive along the way, even if it does come with occasional difficulty.

Perhaps you're familiar with a classic story that truly epitomizes the value of learning from the trials and tribulations of life.

A young woman found herself in an uncomfortable situation: she was kidnapped. As much as she tried, she could not get free from her captor. Her lover, a young man, began a journey to save her. Every time he got just that little bit closer to saving her, he would discover a note that read "the princess is in another castle." This young man, a plumber by trade, was traveling with his brother. Not just regular brothers, it turns out, but Super Mario Brothers. Along their journey, if Luigi fell down a hole, the video game player knew to jump over the hole. If Mario died in a freak accident by walking into a flying turtle with wings, the video game player knew to stomp on the turtle and use its shell as a flying projectile to knock out the other turtles and Goombas. If the gamer were dedicated to the ritual of continuing the adventure, Mario and Princess Peach would be happily reunited at the end of the video game. Only for the Princess to find herself in a similar pickle the next time Nintendo released a game system, of course.

The lesson of this story is to enjoy the journey getting to your end goal. The journey is where you will spend the most time, so make use of every bit of learning you pick up along the way. Let it become a ritual to become tenacious at finding the best rituals to actualize your goal.

Have you ever watched a reality competition talent show? Suspense builds over several weeks as the viewers at home call or text in their votes. By the time the winner is announced, the television end-credits are already rolling. The winner is declared, and there's nowhere for the television program to go. It's the ritual of getting swept up in the melodrama of the competition that keeps us watching for more.

WORK SMART in your business by designing your own rituals. You can model what others have found to be successful, as there's a modern trend of asking what someone's morning rituals are.

I'm now a morning person. I wasn't always one, yet I created a morning ritual that changed my life. I used to believe I was a zombie until noon. I realized I needed more hours of productivity in my business in the early days. Rather than just hoping to tolerate the mornings, I shifted my thinking to reclaim the morning as my sacred, ritualistic time. Be specific to be terrific. If you can clearly define your rituals, the self-ratifying study of what works for you may take on the benefits of self-hypnosis. At night, before I go to sleep, I decide if my morning needs to focus on creation or momentum. If I'm in a creation-mode in my business, my morning includes the music from the "Breakfast Machine Suite," a piece written by Danny Elfman as featured in the movie *Pee-Wee's Big Adventure*. (I wish I were making this up. Go find the song right now, it's an incredible piece of composition.) If my mode will be momentum, it's *If I Had a Million Dollars* by the Canadian rock group, The Barenaked Ladies.

I developed my morning rituals before I picked up a copy of the book *The Miracle Morning: The Not-So-*

Obvious Secret Guaranteed to Transform Your Life (Before 8AM) by Hal Elrod. Check out this incredibly inspirational book to hear how Hal transformed his life by turning his morning into a series of powerful rituals.

Many people come to me for help with weight loss. For example, one woman came into my office with the goal of eating healthier foods and exercising more frequently. We worked together. When she reported back that getting to the gym was effortless, I scanned to see that she'd not been observing the new behavior from a place of novelty. Yes, I want her to be excited at how easily she made the change. However, I've found it's best viewing the exercise from a place of ritual. As if it's something she's always done. Almost on the same brainwave frequencies that she uses to brush her teeth. That is, she's just a person who hits the gym five times a week.

Then again, some business people reach out to me with a rather specific goal. They're not necessarily solving a problem. Perhaps, like an athlete, they're going for performance enhancement. Through the wonders of video web-conferencing platforms, like Skype or Zoom, I worked with an executive client on the west coast of Canada. The goal? That the first two hours of his workday be done in his own peak performance state. His laptop would be on airplane mode blocking all distractions, all web browsers would be closed, and he would zone into his planning for a solid 120 minutes. Rather than observe it as a new habit, he locked it in as if it was a ritual, and he's kept up the momentum many years later.

The most impactful example of rituals comes from the work I've done with athletes. Through hypnosis we can dissolve away distractions, build greater attention to physical specificity, and help you replicate your best strategies. The more skilled the athlete, the more likely they already have well-defined rituals. The method, then, is to apply hypnotic strategies on top of their already-existing rituals. You'll learn "Anchoring" in the WORK SMART strategies later in this book. If they're an amateur, it's more likely that we have to work together to create the ritual while also doing hypnosis. You'll also learn an extremely direct method for "Self-Hypnosis" in the strategies later in this book. I'm going to teach you how to confirm the hypnotic state, then mentally associate your desired outcome. Rather than observing your goal from a dissociated perspective, like watching a movie, you'll instead associate into the scene as if you're already there. You are essentially running the new mental pattern to overwrite the old patterns. This technique is extremely helpful in turning habits into rituals.

Are you picking up the value of getting specific in your strategy? Realize my exact strategies may not be your own. Study the premise and test it out to see what new rituals fit for you. Your rituals may thrive in the evening, while mine start in the morning. You might be that person who plops down in a coffee shop with a laptop or checks into a co-working space for the day. Let it become a human guinea pig experiment to discover what time of day you will hold sacred to create your rituals.

My online calendar is color-coded like a Jackson Pollock painting. Appointments are green. Speaking opportunities are black. Personal events are yellow. Travel is gray. Educational events are orange.

And then there's purple. Purple is power. If something is purple, I'm not allowed to change it. It's blocked off. It's a ritual. The same way I'm at my children's school for a parent-teacher conference, that purple block is sacred. I'm not allowed to change it. If it weren't for those purple blocks, I wouldn't have programs for sale online, and you wouldn't be reading this book.

Harness your most valuable asset and make your time sacred. Make the time for your success, that's when things can really begin to grow.

WORK SMART ACTION STEPS:

☞ Start a list of things you'd like to do more of. Consider balancing the list with professional and personal items. As an experiment, pick an item from each category and commit to doing them with passion and intention for a minimum of ten days. You'll be running new patterns in your mind, respectfully programming in the new behavior.

☞ There's a chapter in the *WORK SMART Strategies* section of this book devoted to Self-Hypnosis. Here's a preview. As your day begins, close your eyes and imagine yourself locking in these new behaviors as if it's always been a part of your life. Mentally step into the experience as if that's what you've always done.

☞ Become a ritual-creating-machine. As you establish what works best for you, keep the momentum going as you create new rituals that keep you focused on the growth of your business.

DESIGN SYSTEMS

You can't do it all yourself, so here's a method to do it all yourself.

I'm about to reveal one of my biggest productivity secrets to you. An easy-to-master method saved my life, enhanced my marriage, and tripled my income along my journey.

I'm going to detail the methods to turn your business efforts into "machines" that you will run and "systems" that operate with ease. If you ever want to increase your business, it can become as easy as pressing a button, and the operation will automatically run as predicted.

Random fun fact: I quit biting my nails thanks to hypnosis almost fifteen years ago. I share this even though it has no correlation to the story I'll tell you about how a nail salon planted the seeds for my financial freedom.

As you move through this chapter, have this question in mind: "What repetitive tasks am I ready to eliminate from my life?" Ask yourself, "What methods have worked the best to grow my business?" We're going to transform these things into systems.

Can the inspirational words from a television infomercial create massive waves in your life, even if you don't buy the product they're pitching? Find out more, right after this commercial break!

I do a lot. I previously described my business life as a "three-ring circus." I see private clients in my hypnosis office most weeks of the year. I publish an industry-specific (micro-niche) podcast that broadcasts ritualistically every Thursday morning. I'm invited to travel and speak around the world. I maintain massive educational communities online.

When I'm recognized at a conference, nearly every time, their dialogue includes the exclamation, "Wow, you're doing a lot these days!" My response is always the same. I smile, and simply respond, "It sure looks that way, doesn't it?"

The principle to "Design Systems" changed my life. I modeled the most successful people that I met in business. I studied what was working for them. I read the books from productivity experts like David Allen and Timothy Ferriss to maximize my time, minimize my efforts, and produce the highest quality experience for my customers. Now, with every task I approach, I'll ask myself, "How can I do this once" or "How can I streamline this to make it easier?"

Technologies change from year-to-year, so I'll refrain from turning this chapter into a laundry list of website recommendations for services that might disappear by the time you read this book. Let's focus instead on the principles for "Design Systems," as they will apply universally even as the technology world evolves.

Imagine turning on your television early in the morning. A man wearing an apron appears on the screen. He loads a raw, whole chicken onto a metal stick, which is exactly the image you wanted to see to start your day. This friendly man with a sincere smile, conveying his excitement is absolutely genuine, loads the meat into a toaster-oven shaped box. As if he and the audience had been rehearsing it for hours, he asks the live audience, "What's the next step?" In perfect unison, the entire space roars with an enthusiastic "SET IT AND FORGET IT!"

Ron Popeil closed the door on his Showtime Rotisserie Grill, turned a dial, and walked away. Within a few hours, the door would open to what promised to be the most perfectly cooked chicken you could ever make in your own home. The infomercial sold over eight million units and generated more than a billion dollars.

The catchphrase of the product changed the direction of my life. How can I apply the physical and mental ease of "Set it and forget it" to both my business and personal life?

When I launched my local hypnosis business, I was inspired by a conversation with a local business coach. A point of frustration she expressed became an "away-from" motivation system for me, driving me to realize, again like a television infomercial, "there's got to be a better way!"

She expressed that she loved meeting with new clients. A new client would mean she could directly help transform the shape of their business and their life. A new client meant money in the bank as she'd get paid for her services. Her only complaint was that it took so long to send a new client their first-session homework plus driving directions to her office.

This conflict opened my eyes to a flaw in her business systems. She explained that her welcome email to a new client had to include specific driving directions as her office was through a private entrance on the side of her home. They had to know exactly where to park. There were instructions about an email attachment they needed to print and complete by hand.

I was inspired to overhaul my office strategies. I crafted new welcome emails and office forms for my clients that evening. Other than a change-of-address, when I moved my office, and several rate increases over the years, the welcome email and office forms are the same nearly ten years later. The coach was spending forty-five minutes completing this office administrative task. In my world, an automation sequence from a drop-down menu took care of it. I shared what I had done with the coach, and she's now using the same principle in her life.

To "Design Systems" doesn't always have to be a technical adventure with online automation. When I do a keynote presentation for a business or professional organization, the program is templated and modular, so I can put the pieces together that address the goals of their team. I teach a number of strategies to internalize goals, one of which is self-hypnosis, which I demonstrate with volunteers from their audience. Depending on the event, I can piece together the best strategies to teach that align with their business environment. Another system is in place at the time of booking the speech, as a brief "needs analysis" system is employed conversationally with the executive team to identify their goals and set the objectives for the presentation. The program is easily custom-designed to match the needs of the client. Just like the story of the welcome email and office forms for a private client, the contracts and travel arrangements follow a similar systematic journey.

Ron Popeil was right. "Set it and forget it."

Systems allow you to model yourself. The majority of my business now comes from fully-automated online activity. I frequently share seminars through "exclusive online learning events." That's a much better title than the tech-jargon of calling it a "webinar." While you read the method of this presentation, realize the principles can be applied to any aspect of your business that needs systematization.

The strength of a webinar is that it's a timely online event. People sign up online to receive a series of messages counting down to the date. They receive the attendance access link and then a follow-up series sharing the replays and resources. From one email signup, to be a part of the event, you have permission to send a number of checkpoints in communication. Lead with value. My goal is to help my audience produce a small win through learning something new. This easily transitions into a polite promotion for a product or service that will help the viewer create an even larger win.

Here are some examples of this education-to-conversion. I taught you a self-hypnosis technique to dissolve a craving? Please come to my office to knock out the entire smoking habit. You learned how to take your personal service and expand it to groups? Please purchase my complete business training. I taught you a mental trigger to provoke your own organic state of confidence? Please have me come share it with your staff. Abolish the mindset of this conversation being an "upsell." Think of it as an "upgrade" to naturally pivot from education to offer.

Here's where the systems come in. Every step of the process is automated. Every email of the sequence is pre-written before the first promotional email invite is broadcast. The countdown emails and subsequent replay sequence were programmed on schedule in advance. The benefit here is that your messages will all now carry a congruent tone of voice through the sequence, plus you won't forget to do it later.

I had a programmer build this automation system for me years ago. Every new event is a model of a previous one. My task is to produce the new video program and present it. My team's task is to create new graphics and change the name of the event and dates in the email sequences. This allows me to put my complete focus toward putting on an outstanding learning event.

Set it and forget it.

I strive to make the experience provide genuine value for the attendees. I can focus on sharing 100% value in this permission-based platform. To be transparent, my welcome emails state, "Yes, I will be promoting an upcoming training opportunity. However, I know you'll benefit from the content I'm going to share during the program." It's no surprise that the end of the presentation pivots to an offer to get more. I also only allow myself to continue contact with the attendees who haven't yet purchased if I'm continuing to provide value. "Here's a download of the presentation" or "Here's that document I promised you." Value first, followed by "only four spots are left." Lead with value. Your buyers will thank you for the experience.

I run this "webinar machine" system several times a year to print money. I hope you've already noticed that these WORK SMART principles can stand on their own, yet they become more powerful as you combine them with others. Having created this powerful system, my team duplicates an older campaign, changes the titles, images, and dates, and we'll run the machine again to another audience with different content for the next event.

Team. I've used that word a few times now. Did you catch it? That word is magic.

Is your business bursting at the seams? Are you struggling because you're behind schedule, trying to complete too many tasks, and, unfortunately, dropping the ball in several parts of your life? It's time now to reveal the #1 thing that changed the shape of my life.

Let's talk about outsourcing so you can become the wizard behind the curtain rather than the jack of all trades. Have you found yourself sitting at a computer for hours in a state of frustration because you could not figure out some piece of software? Embrace this frustration as your cue to hire someone else to help you!

Just because you can, doesn't mean you should.

In my previous arts management career, I learned how to operate professional sound design software. I also learned how to rapidly build websites and maintain them. These are essential skills in the businesses I operate. However, my time is better spent speaking to business groups, developing new programs, working with private clients, and spending time with my family. I designed systems in my life to hand off the technical tasks to someone else so my time may now be focused on the things that will scale up my business. Refuse to be a slave to your business and allow your business to now work for you.

Want an added bonus? The expert can handle the software better than you can.

My podcast is one of my systems. New content releases every week like clockwork. Sometimes it's a solo session where I teach something. Other times, we capture a recorded conversation with someone I feel my audience needs to meet. The initial recording is completed and immediately saved in Dropbox. This folder is already synced with the filesharing service to my audio editors. They have the file within seconds of my hitting save. I produce another recording to capture my opening remarks, an introduction with a soft promotion for my programs, and the closing statements. I click save and, within seconds, it's automatically uploaded to the Dropbox account of my editors, too. They handle the editing, perform magical things to make recorded voices sound better, and upload it into the production cycle for release.

While this system is running, so is another system. The team of writers produces the first draft of the show notes. They save it into our shared Dropbox folder, and I receive an alert when it's ready for my edits. It takes me less than five minutes to make a few adjustments, saving the final version in the shared folder. This automatically flies through the digital cloud to my web & graphic designer who prepares images and the website to promote the recording.

These are people I've been working with for at least two years. This next fact may surprise you. We don't talk to each other. We don't have to. There are occasional "Hello" messages or "Happy birthday" notes and the rare "My guest's phone rang during the interview, can you edit it out?" We don't need to directly speak to each other. We don't have to. It's a system that now runs on its own. My responsibility is focused on producing valuable experiences for my audience, applying a few finishing touches, and listening to the program with everyone else when it releases on schedule.

The systems go even deeper than that. This program releases on schedule every week. However, this isn't a weekly task. I batch produce these programs. Remember the purple calendar entries? Just once or twice a month I'll set aside time to record, typically producing programs well over a month in advance of public release.

Set it and forget it.

Whether it's something you design for yourself or hire an outsourcer to build some automation for you, you empower yourself to WORK SMART. No longer will you need to metaphorically bash your head on a computer desk because of a lack of technical skill.

Start with the user experience. Work as if you're not going to touch any computers or software at all. You will be responsible for some effort in communication and content creation, though this creator-only mindset will put your focus where it ought to be. Focus your efforts on the user experience.

My most profitable projects began as drawings on blank sheets of paper. A pencil sketch on the back of an envelope generated $40,000 of new business. I've built websites and designed multi-step online educational programs with this method, even though I've got a reputation of crashing my own websites because I thought I could fix them. I design best in a "bare bones" environment: a single-color pen on a white sheet of paper. I do my best writing in the Notepad or TextEdit applications on a computer. If I'm not allowed to change the fonts or size of the text, my 100% focus is on crafting the written message.

Avoid the distraction of making it pretty. That comes later.

I can now pass the work off to someone with the necessary skills to turn the idea into a reality. As outsourcing is sometimes an international dialogue, my preferred method is to "show" rather than "tell." I'll make a video with my smartphone explaining the project or use screen-recording software like Camtasia to describe the task. I'll talk through the project and upload the video privately online.

Remember these magic words: "Make this pretty."

You might even begin with a model to emulate. It's important to not rip off someone else's idea, though their ideas may inspire you. My local hypnosis business website was modeled from the website of a nail salon in California. I'm not in the business of doing manicures and pedicures. Not yet, at least. However, the layout of nail salon's site clearly featured their top three services. Everything else was in a drop-down menu called "Other." Their website inspired a pen-and-paper sketch, and my design team built something new from the ground up. I'd bet the nail salon wouldn't even recognize any hint of their website that inspired my site!

This method of modeling is a model of other models. Disney's *The Lion King* is a retelling of William Shakespeare's *Hamlet*. The George Clooney movie *Oh Brother, Where Art Thou?* is an adaptation of Homer's

The Odyssey. A friend of mine once worked writing for afternoon soap operas and children's cartoons. Imagine the massive number of scripts they would have to produce! He shared the story that one time he literally threw a dart at a bookcase full of classical works of literature. He found a theme in a story that seemed interesting and adapted the conflict for the characters in his script.

Here are your other magic words: "Make me one like this."

Keep your focus on the service or product you expertly provide while others expertly handle the technology. Where do you find these people? I recommend using your local network or exploring peer-reviewed outsourcing website communities. At the time of this printing, I've found the best service from the website Upwork.

Unfortunately, I've met people who would now turn off at the mention of outsourcing. They cry out, "I've tried that, and it didn't work for me." Remember, it's very rarely the platform, it's almost always the strategy.

The mistake I often see people make is they jump into the task too quickly. They metaphorically try to consummate the outsourcing relationship before the first date. Take them out for coffee before getting too intimate!

Start with a micro-task. Do you need a new website? Start your process earlier in the relationship as you hire someone capable of web design to help you build a logo. Consider this task your first date as you learn about their responsiveness. Now you can decide whether to continue the relationship. Expand the job to request a graphic design of a new website: just the design, not the actual build. Perhaps now expand to having them build out the navigation menu and home page, now the entire site.

Remember the Bill Murray movie *What About Bob?* Dr. Leo Marvin was right: BABY STEPS! If the person you've hired becomes unreliable or unable to follow instruction, you have the ability to exit the situation before it became a relationship. Politely exit the contract, pay for the services already rendered, and hire someone new. The benefit of peer-reviewed sites like Upwork is that you can explore a person's reviews and portfolio even before hiring.

How do you make payment? I suggest starting with pay-by-assignment tasks. Offer a specific rate for a logo, then a specific rate for the full site. As you're now satisfied with their quality of work, pivot the relationship into a by-the-hour role as needed. Here's a life-changing strategy: pay them for their time to connect via web-conference software like Skype or Zoom to share their screen and teach you how to make small updates to your website. This may be helpful for simple tasks like updating a blog or adding a quick thank you page. Deepen the relationship by pivoting into a monthly contract. Having a relationship with an ongoing outsourcer expedites your process as you further systematize your business. My programmer and I can launch a new membership product online in a single day. I can share a photo with my designer, and she nails the podcast design for a Facebook ad for a class on the first draft. I also don't have to spend my time looking for new people to help me!

My favorite outsourcing story was the time I attempted to update the layout on one of my websites. I was up early one morning and felt inspired. "I can probably do the task myself faster than I can send the design notes," I unfortunately believed. I crashed the entire website. I frantically sent S.O.S. messages to my programmer who fixed the issue in minutes. She also temporarily locked me out of my own website because "you keep screwing it up, and this is why you pay me." Some people would be offended by this action and end the contract. I gave her a raise.

"I can't afford to outsource" is an objection I often hear. I'll reply you can't afford not to outsource. I trust you've already realized the value of outsourcing from the stories I've shared with you. In addition to the value, please let it become a balance of priorities. I'm amazed by people who will spend $5,000 on flights, hotels, and convention registration to attend a conference but will not give someone $40 to make their business card look decent. Pay yourself first to reinvest in your success.

The value of including outsourcing in this "Design Systems" dialogue is that you don't have to fall into the virus of "Superhero Syndrome." Break past the expectation that you have to do it all yourself. The brick wall of "I don't know how to do that" becomes an incredible doorway to letting someone else make your ideas better. Given the shape of your business, everything I've shared with you can also translate to hiring additional staff either part-time or full-time.

Thinking of your business as a series of systems helps you to know where you are at all points of your entrepreneurial journey. Remember the story from the "Print Money" chapter when my webhosting company was hacked? I ran the system of getting out into my community and networking. Think in terms of systems, and you will know how to turn your business on and off.

Building systems allows you to duplicate yourself. Empower yourself to exponentially increase your productivity and your income. WORK SMART by spending time working less. Focus your time on scaling up your business or time with your family.

The real question: what's working, what's not working, and what can you hand off to someone else?

WORK SMART ACTION STEPS:

☞ What would it be like to create an employee manual for yourself? Designing systems doesn't have to only be a technical task involving software and a virtual team. Like the story of revisiting network marketing when my websites crashed, I knew exactly what to do to turn my business back on. Track the efforts necessary that make each part of your business WORK SMART more consistently.

☞ Run the imaginary exercise of dividing your business personality into a few dozen hypothetical parts. Some of these potential "parts" could include doing your service, producing your product, promoting your work, updating your website, responding to emails, and taking care of your own accounting. These parts of you are your "staff." Make a note of which parts absolutely MUST be done by you. The threat of "downsizing" or "layoffs" can be terrifying if you're an employee. However, it's exhilarating as an entrepreneur! Fire yourself for the tasks that don't 100% require you!

☞ Start small. Re-read the outsourcing system I outlined to start with a micro-task and evolve it into a relationship. Your physical or virtual staff may be skilled technicians, but they're not psychics. A principle of hypnotic communication is "the meaning of the communication is the response it gets." Recognize that you will have a learning curve to best express what you want a job to be.

☞ Take good care of the people you work with. Put the words "please" and "thank you" in your instructions as you communicate. Send the occasional bonus for a job well done. They may be your staff, but they're still people. They will help you design an incredible lifestyle for yourself, so be sure they know you appreciate their work.

SCALE UP

The world has become a lot smaller. It's never been easier to pivot a small business into a global brand. Let's talk about growth. You're about to learn to WORK SMART in order to "Scale Up."

In this chapter, you'll find methods to expand your business beyond the nine-to-five lifestyle. Thanks to the systems you've designed in the previous chapter, you'll be able to focus your time strictly on those things you enjoy doing to continue the growth of your business year-after-year.

What got you started in business may not be the mechanism that helps you to grow. Just like a baby that has to figure out how to crawl before it can stand up and walk, you'll WORK SMART in your thinking to evolve your business to the next phase of your own success.

We'll talk about the mindset of hunting dollars rather than chasing down pennies, how to overcome competitive self-imposed limitations, and the ability to convert your knowledge into a passive income project that earns you money while you sleep.

To "Scale Up" is to reach new audiences and increase the value you share with your clients. By providing more opportunities for your value, you create more opportunities to receive value in return. You earn more money.

This is an important distinction: provide more value as you receive more value. Operate your business from a place of integrity; you'll create an irreplaceable brand that may keep your business growing as long as you like.

Remember the filter of "more of the same or scale up?" Look at the steps you take in your business to gauge whether your efforts will keep you producing similar results or continue to grow greater success.

Be aware that it's all right to keep that status quo if that's what you want. You may have built your business to operate at the specific level of your own choosing. It's fine to embrace that. There's one segment of my business that is basically on autopilot. It's not my desire to release it or increase it. It's a segment of live programs that I've mostly "retired" myself from doing by subcontracting these events. The income benefits the people I hire, the clients remain satisfied, and it provides another flow of income on top of everything else I'm doing.

Keep up what you're doing if you want to keep up what you're doing. One of my consulting clients was already operating a business in which she saw, at a minimum, thirty-five private clients a week. We talked through the steps of product creation, design, and promotion to expand her passive income business. She successfully launched several new programs. When we were through working, she gave me the biggest hug and said something that surprised and inspired me. The experience helped her validate that her true passion was working one-to-one with her clients. She loved the learning and received the unexpected benefit of realizing it was time to raise her rates. I see no conflict with this. She was already extremely successful in her business endeavors, and she realized she loved things as they were. If it ain't broke, right?

Let's bring it back to your story. Where do you want things to grow? Where do you want more freedom? There's a danger in working strictly in a dollars-for-hours model. It can wear you down. It can leave you in a business where you're stuck only earning an income if you're physically there doing the job. People who live this way often fear taking vacations. They avoid situations in which they could miss out on business. They live by their phone and have a hard time shutting down to relax. They position their lives to be dependent on a week-to-week or month-to-month lifestyle.

Retirement is never a choice and time off is rarely an option for them. They're stuck working for their own business. The opportunity to step away and enjoy the later years of life is a fantasy to those who positioned themselves so that their livelihood depends on the next payment. The exception to this is the old saying that "if you love what you're doing, you never work a day in your life." Let's be honest. Some days it's work. Some days it's a job. The opportunity to "Scale Up" allows you to step away from the requirements of a standard workweek. If you stick with a dollars-for-hours model of business, the only opportunities are to either work more hours or charge more money. This can be done, but it can wear on you.

Systems are the key to scaling up. As you view your business from the perspective of building systems, you empower your time to branch out and build up. Know where your current business is coming from, know where the money is already flowing in, and know where to duplicate it. As you build an entrepreneurial adventure that easily runs on its own, it's easier to let your current state of business run like a machine so you can explore new opportunities.

Develop your systems to the point that you know what works best for success. Scaling up is easy as you know when and where to duplicate yourself. You know where to spend your time and money. The phone rings at my hypnosis office. Someone is trying to sell me a print ad for a newspaper in the community. I'm able to politely decline because my systems have already demonstrated where my ideal clients come from. Putting my business out to the general community in a non-targeted way hasn't worked in my experience. Be specific to be terrific. A print ad would just deliver "more of the same" rather than the opportunity to "Scale Up."

That doesn't mean the interaction is over. There may be a benefit to pivot the conversation to what personal development columns they're currently featuring. This is the exact situation I created years ago to write a monthly column for a local newspaper. The visibility and credibility of the article were much more valuable than another advertisement. This reinforces the lesson of "Be the expert, not the vendor." The entire WORK SMART way of thinking moved into full throttle as I printed color copies of the articles and mailed them to influencers and decision-makers in my community. Build assets and leverage them!

As you "Scale Up," consider the classic 80/20 principle. Frequently 80% of your success comes from 20% of what you do. Scaling requires the decision to let go of the bottom percentage of your business. This is a bit of a leap as it may mean letting some income streams go. You could alternatively job this work out as I previously mentioned or bring on additional staff. What got you started may not keep you growing.

Just because you're good at something doesn't mean you have to do it for the rest of your life. I loved my theater job, but I knew when it was time to go. I loved traveling the country and working with public schools, but the long hours on the road didn't mesh with my personal goals. I still occasionally do these motivational programs at schools, though, most often, I now subcontract it out.

The trigger to "Scale Up" sometimes is that your message needs a bigger audience. I used to host a local MeetUp group. This event was always free. I would put out coffee, tea, snacks, and often pay the guest speakers a respectable amount of money to be a featured speaker. The attendees never were asked to pay for their attendance.

Another group met a few miles away. They had a reputation of being predatory in making sure every attendee paid $10 to cover their event's expense. My focus was elsewhere. By hosting a quality networking group and by welcoming people into a positive environment, the venture was indirectly profitable. Because of the visibility and the quality experiences I produced, people became my private clients or invested in my training programs. A single night's event could result in $10,000 or more.

Where would you rather focus? $10 a head or $10,000 in total? Don't let the pennies distract you from the dollars.

Place value on the soft skills that you gained from your start-up years. My programs for high school events built the presentational foundation necessary to now speak in the corporate world. The previous career of management in professional theater prepared me for the mindset of automation and the integrity of delivering the same high-value presentation, even if it's the hundredth time I've done it. Embrace the skills and strengths you've gained to leverage these as assets well into your future.

The seed for this "Scale Up" mentality was planted when I hosted the MeetUp group. While the attendees were outstanding people and good friends of mine, I was looking at the same faces each month. I wanted to reach a bigger audience. This was my catalyst to start to podcast, write, speak, shoot videos, and attend conferences. This also shifted the focus of my business away from one-to-one to one-to-many.

Will broadcasting a message to a larger audience dilute the power of your message? My experience is the opposite. I've expanded my reach to people who get to know the work I do, and I sold more training or personal services. You'll discover the mental triggers that make this possible in the "Lead Generation" chapter.

If you are providing a valuable experience, I would suggest that it is your ethical responsibility to scale up your business! Serve a larger audience and expand the reach of your message. Take a moment to brainstorm how what you do could be adapted for a larger audience. Increasing your reach will help more people discover you. The other benefit is that they'll already be in rapport with you by the time they make personal contact. Your value increases as a result. You've heard of a sales funnel. I call this "Positioning yourself at the end of the funnel."

Some people in business are held back from scaling by the fear that someone else is out there providing a similar service. Why does there need to be another version? Why would someone buy from me? Check out the book *Strive: Your Life is Short, Pursue What Matters* from author Tim Hiller. He writes, "Don't compare your beginning to someone else's middle." People need to hear your story. People need your variation on a common theme. Plus, we all start somewhere. That person you may be comparing yourself to also had to start somewhere. Just get started, establish momentum, and focus on doing things to the best of your abilities.

"Scale Up" by networking with others. Surround yourself with a community of people who are also successfully growing their businesses. Keep an eye out for the opportunity to partner on new projects. The business of a co-production will expand your reach to new audiences. You can leverage your skills or services to new industries in a symbiotic relationship.

A catchphrase from the vaudeville days of entertainment was "The amateur changes their act. The professional changes their audience." Some performers would become massively skilled at just one thing and tour the world only with an eight-minute act. By networking with another business owner, you take your "act" to a brand-new audience.

There is also incredible value in knowledge. There's a renaissance of information-products these days as people are hungry for information that works. If you can shortcut someone's learning curve, they happily trade their money for your experience. Capture the information you've gathered into a product you could likely sell for the rest of your life. Modern technology has made it incredibly simple to create information-on-demand products. Affordable video cameras and high-quality microphones are readily available.

There's likely a book inside you waiting to be written. There's something of value you could teach in a series of videos. Take your experiences out of your office and onto a platform as you speak about what you do. Hire someone to build you a website. The knowledge you have can change the lives of others around the world.

Want an easy system to produce educational content? One of my strategies is to do a "video shoot disguised as a live class." I teach my business strategies or hypnosis methodology in a live event while the cameras are rolling. The students in the room benefit from the event, then we can spin the content into a passive income product. A friend and I produced a large class together in Las Vegas. We sold out the event with about three-dozen attendees. We had rave reviews from the students in attendance, and the income was exceptional. In addition to the students, three cameras were rolling to capture the event. We had the content professionally edited and continue to sell this program today.

"But then people will know how to do what I do!" I hear that as a concern from some people. "I don't want to saturate my market or create competition." This is scarcity thinking. While I make it a point to arm my students with all the knowledge necessary to take action, many of them become my best referral sources. I also adopt a mindset of transparency and abundance as I step into the role of educator. I have been known to teach the step-by-step methods of what's working "right now" in my business. I explain this opinion in my courses as "You can't do it the way that I've done it." I intend no arrogance with this statement, as the next message is that "You shouldn't do it the way that I've done it. Take these principles and strategies and make them your own." Teaching both specifics as well as the philosophy beneath the specifics empowers someone else in business to bring in their own personal style, skills, and character. Be yourself, not somebody else.

"Scale up" your business while you maintain your business. Thanks to the systems you've built in the previous chapters, it's the strategy of continuing to level up your success and keep the parts of the business you're the most passionate about.

It's time to think bigger about what you can achieve. Set some big goals to reach a larger and perhaps more premium audience and take action now.

WORK SMART ACTION STEPS:

☞ Consider who your ideal audience is for the product or service you provide. Brainstorm a bit to figure out what industries have similar needs and explore who you know in your current network that can help you make contact to expand into a new market. Both you and your new partner receive a credibility boost by working together to better serve a specific need. Build a list of people you know and start to brainstorm some joint promotions.

☞ "Scale Up" with systems. In addition to my speaking, I've been invited to teach a "Self-Hypnosis for Internalizing Goals" workshop at business events. One of my private clients expressed a need to reduce conflict amongst his staff of medical administrators. I made a few adjustments to the corporate program to transform it into a stress-relief program for his staff. Take an inventory of your current offerings and realize that with only a few changes, you can morph what you do into a product for a different audience.

☞ You now have two lists: influencers and assets. Schedule some phone calls or live meetings to discuss the idea of enhancing each other's businesses by combining efforts. Set deadlines to keep the two of you on task and provide an outstanding experience for a new audience.

HARNESS LEAD GENERATION

No matter what line of work you're in, I want you to focus on selling just one thing.

Are you a real estate agent? Do you work in insurance? Do you have a specific skill like being a photographer, painter, or website designer? Are you a speaker or perhaps even a hypnotist like me?

What if I told you the secret to harnessing the most powerful of sales principles came down to selling the same thing, no matter what industry you're in? Again, no matter your line of business, there's only one thing you should focus on selling.

From my start-up to scale up story, you're going to learn the one product (which isn't even a product!) that you should focus your efforts on selling. Together, we'll rethink the "sales funnel" model through the value of relationships. I'll detail my methods to establish a business that easily attracts the specific people with whom you'd like to work. You'll learn how to easily navigate people through a successful customer journey.

What's that "one thing" you should be selling? Keep reading to learn more.

Let's bring the story back to November 2003. There was a girl at my college that I wanted to get to know better. Imagine how well things would have gone if I had walked up to her and proudly announced, "You and I are going to have children!" It might not have gone well. Then again, after having been married to her for more than ten years and now having a better understanding of her sense of humor, it might have worked.

While this chapter is about the value of a specific method of marketing called "lead generation," it's really a focus on creating better relationships. Most people drive their business through a "direct response" method of marketing. They broadcast a sales message and hope people will buy after one or several repeated interactions.

Here's a product. Here's the price. Do you want it? How about now? I would never suggest that this method doesn't work. It does, though it may require more effort and patience. It can sometimes become a numbers game. "If I just make the offer to more people, perhaps I'll sell more." It can also be more difficult to offer a product at a premium rate.

The lead generation marketing style builds sustainability and automatically trains you to build your business in the form of systems. When you try to sell to everybody, you often end up selling to nobody. Instead, metaphorically, and sometimes literally, have people raise their hand to express an interest in the product or service you offer. Now you spend your time only with those people, the "leads," who have already expressed an interest in what you do.

It's time to rethink the "sales funnel" model. As your potential customers metaphorically travel down the funnel deeper into a business relationship with you, you continue to expand rapport and demonstrate value. This is paramount. Put value at every step of the journey. Rather than thinking in terms of SELLING, you create a potential journey of adding more VALUE the deeper they travel down the metaphorical funnel. Here's the amazing benefit: you will be inspiring your ideal clients to take action, and you will be allowing those who are not yet a fit for what you do to politely exit the process on their own. You need not be fearful of becoming a dreaded "salesperson." This business model focuses your efforts on EDUCATING rather than SELLING.

I suggest the best form of lead generation is driven by creating valuable content your potential clients will benefit from. Content can take the form of a video on a website, an article, a speech given in your community, or even the still-viable methods of business cards and paper brochures. The first step of lead generation begins with delivering a valuable experience which establishes visibility in your market and starts a system of reciprocity. If your free information is this good, imagine how it gets better when they step into a business relationship with you!

Establish the ability to the stay in contact with your audience. You'll ignite the #1 secret method of many successful businesses: the list! Your market and your product will help you define your delivery mechanism. I see the same good results through email marketing thanks to automation tools like AWeber, GetReponse, or Infusionsoft. It's not the platform, it's the strategy. You can also do this for social media groups, text message marketing, and even postal mail.

You will deepen the lead generation relationship when your future client "purchases" further information by providing their contact information (most often an email address). A simple online search, or the resources of the email automation provider you choose, will give you the current ethical and legal guidelines for permission-based marketing messages.

"But I hate receiving marketing messages in my email!" I hear some of you already cry. I've got an easy solution for you. Don't do it badly. Seriously, it's that simple. Like anything else out there in the business world, many good methods get a bad reputation thanks to people who are sloppy in their methods. I know someone who hurt their professional reputation by harvesting emails from websites and sending unsolicited bulk sales emails to people without permission. That's the definition of spam! Keep contact only with those to whom you have permission to broadcast a message and keep your focus on providing more and more VALUE rather than only sending sales offers.

Provide more value to get more value. There's no set rule or exact pattern you must follow. Consider sending three or four pieces of valuable content to balance out one direct sales message. Timing is critical, as I'll aim to only run one or two promotions a month. If all you're doing is sending "buy now" messages, people will quickly start to opt out of your list. These are likely the emails you hate receiving, right? So don't do it that way!

When I suggest you lead with value, realize you can also put an offer "below the fold." This terminology dates back to newspapers, where a headline would be at the top of the newspaper, with content beneath the fold of the newspaper. Imagine the layout of an attention-grabbing email subject line: a positive instruction to interact with something that will benefit the reader; perhaps a link to a video. Beneath that something like "Want more like this? Click here to learn about my program." It's a much more natural way of strengthening the business relationship rather than going directly for the sale.

This is exactly what has built for me what is now a million-dollar brand. Build the ultimate system to drive the exponential growth of your business. I maintain a schedule of providing free content. This guides people further down the sales funnel by providing value with an offer to take the next step in our relationship. My list grows every month, and my sales continue to grow.

For those of you with local brick-and-mortar businesses, stay with me here as this isn't just an online business strategy. A friend of mine, a chef, built a loyal following for his restaurant by using stories featuring his staff and the history of his original recipes. His readers developed a deeper relationship with him, and many of them dine at his location on a regular basis now.

I've used a similar method to drive attention to my local hypnosis business. I'm teaching helpful methods to rapidly dissolve stress, sharing tips on public speaking, or even giving insight on how to let go of your own fears. I provide value first. My office schedule easily fills.

You can also deepen the relationship for your lead generation by providing a high-value experience at a lower cost than the core offer of your business. Often called a "tripwire," it's an effective strategy to grow your business and get paid while doing it. I teach a week-long training course, and I'll frequently offer a one-day introductory sampler class for those that are curious. The attendees receive a ton of value from the one-day experience. Those ready to move forward in the relationship sign up for the full experience. Thanks to list segmentation in my email systems, the people who have attended the one-day event receive a different level of communication about the full course as they're already deeper into the relationship.

I just mentioned your "core offer." This is your primary product or service. You might have several different offerings. If you're a service-based business, this is the action of going and performing the service. If you're selling a product, the product itself may be your core offer. When I spoke before of direct response marketing, this is where many businesses put their focus. They make a direct offer for you to buy their product or service. If you insist on sticking with a direct response model, at least start to put out valuable content to demonstrate the value of your core offer. This also cultivates community, as people will start to follow your brand.

Consider the story that began this chapter. The relationship with my wife first had to start by asking her out on a date. We eventually moved in together. We then got a cat. Then I proposed. We then got married. Then we bought a house. Then we got a dog. Then we had a daughter. Then we moved to a bigger house. Then we had a son. We recently celebrated ten years of marriage together. Imagine your prospective client relationship following the arc of a romantic relationship, and you'll better understand your business efforts. Asking a stranger to immediately buy a thousand-dollar product may be just as successful as asking someone you've just met to go half-in on a thirty-year home mortgage and to trade off whose turn it is that week to scoop the cat's litter box. I hope some of you are realizing why previous attempts to grow your business may not have worked!

The relationship arc is the foundation when I speak at an event. I'll deliver value to the attendees during my presentation. I'll make an offer to continue the relationship by sending resources by email. Some of the attendees will follow me to a vendor area where they will purchase my programs. Others will continue to receive value by way of content sent by an automated email stream or private access to a membership area on my website. There will be the value received at the actual live event, though the real income is created by the long-term relationship we're building.

The lead generation method allows you to add more steps to guide people to your core offers. You have a greater opportunity to grow your business. You may even discover places to further expand your business by maximizing the opportunities and needs of people who have already taken your core offer. Private coaching? A mastermind group? Deepen the value of the relationship, and you deepen the opportunity to create and receive more value.

Do you know the premise of the velvet rope? Only select people are welcomed into the elite restaurant or private club. If you think of your lead generation methods as a velvet rope, you no longer need to be the person standing there at the entry point of your business. Automation emails, online videos, and other valuable content will handle the selection process for you. Your potential audience will qualify or disqualify themselves in making a buying decision. You potentially negate all buyer's remorse as those taking action will know exactly what they're purchasing. This is a good thing: you're helping your potential client make the best decision.

This is illustrated by a story of my corporate speaking. I teach the audience three strategies to internalize goals in my presentation. One of them happens to be self-hypnosis, which I demonstrate with volunteers from the group. During the sound-check, a man in the organization walked up to me and informed me that he was not going to be a volunteer.

"Have you seen a program like mine before?" I asked. He replied that he had not. I briefly explained that there's full audience participation at the beginning of the event for people to discover the power of their own subconscious minds out in their own seats. It's only after everyone has experienced entertaining hypnotic phenomena that I invite volunteers to come onto the platform. I playfully told him, "You haven't had the first experience in the audience yet, so I don't think you're qualified yet to make that decision." He laughed at this, and guess whose hand was the first in the air when I called for someone from the audience!

Model this story. The hypnosis is just an anecdote of this lesson. Put anybody on a stage asking for a volunteer. Why are so many reluctant to come on stage? Perhaps it's not the fear of being in front of so many people. It's more likely because the speaker hasn't yet given them a reason or benefit to volunteer. Give people a reason to take action, and more of them will take action. I gave the volunteer in this story a reason to come on stage. If he had kept his original decision-making criteria, he would have missed out on the experience.

Design your systems for lead generation so you set the criteria for making a buying decision. Do this as a favor to the customer. They're likely entering into a unique venture doing business with you. If you can provide the map to make the right decision, you're making their lives easier.

I'm a hypnotist. There are some people out there with fears or misconceptions of the process. Rather than being a loss of control, we're creating a heightened awareness that they can change their own habits and feelings. My sales process must demonstrate through education how the process actually plays out. In addition to that, it's most likely a service they've never purchased. What other questions should they ask beyond "How many sessions?" and "How much is it?" I've created a guide for them to know what credentials are important and how to find if the practitioner they're researching has a proven track-record. You know the criteria that are important in your line of business. It's your ethical responsibility to let your audience know.

I foreshadowed that the key to a successful business comes down to selling one thing. Ready the drumroll. It's time to reveal the "one thing." The game changes when you discover the secret product that all your business systems should be designed to sell: THE NEXT STEP.

When you focus on selling the next step along the journey, your focus is naturally on deepening the quality of your relationship to your buyer. Remember the list of life events that led to ten years of marriage? Buying a home together and getting pets seemed like a logical progression toward having kids. You can break down your entire business into these "next step" mentalities.

The subject line of an email sells the next step of opening the message. The images and layout inside the email sell the next step of reading the email. The links within the message sell the next step of clicking and watching a video. An appropriate attention-grabbing statement in the first ten seconds of the video sells the next step of watching the entire sequence. The more likely I am to succeed in these baby steps along the journey, the more likely my audience will go through the steps necessary to purchase. Purchasing one of my online programs will more likely sell the next step of private consulting.

Why are you learning this from a hypnotist? Because that's how hypnosis works. It's a process of compounding levels of heightened receptivity in the mind. It's a natural experience in which more profound hypnotic phenomena are possible the deeper someone moves through the process. In my demonstrations, perhaps there's the moment where someone has their eyes open looking at their own arm, and it's magical as the more they try to bend it, they cannot. Deeper into the experience, I can suggest a negative hallucination as if I were to physically disappear. In terms of hypnotic technique, I know the negative hallucination requires a more profound depth of hypnosis than the experience of the stiff arm. Even without hypnosis training, you can now guess that I'd want to have produced the stiff-arm phenomenon to know I can proceed with the mental vanishing stunt.

The core of my presentations is to use a memorable experience to drive home a teaching point. When you change the picture in your mind that it's a steel bar rather than your own arm, you can accept the hypnotic suggestion as if it couldn't bend. Imagine if you now change the picture in your mind to see yourself as a successful business person. What can now begin to happen for you? There is an abundance of business opportunities waiting to be had. The negative hallucination experience demonstrates how to avoid the situation of missing out on business that's been in front of you the whole time.

Examine how this "next step" philosophy is the foundation of my speaking. I used a valuable experience to drive home a teaching point. Heighten attention before making an important statement. Your communication is always influential, so I suggest you make it impactful.

Ask yourself what "next step" would be the most appropriate to assist your customer in making a buying decision. It requires some creativity as you design your systems. Once you know the logical progression of the relationship with your customer, you know how to build more lead generation steps for people to build relationships with you through your funnels. This takes the stress out of running a business. Lead with education, inform your potential client, build stronger connections, and you'll build a solid business.

Now, your task is to put this into action. Start to build your systems to grow your business. Use the principle to WORK SMART designing the journey your clients will take. Start with the end in mind and stay client-centered with the process. Think through each step along the lead generation journey, so you help your buyer achieve several small wins. Empower them to become more informed each step of the way. Ask yourself, "How can I demonstrate value?" The valuable experiences you are designing will naturally position you as the authority you are in your industry without the need to brag or boast.

There's science to this. These small wins may produce positive results in their brain chemistry. The success they achieve along their journey helps to ride that dopamine rush, a feel-good hormone within the mind and body, which encourages them to move on to the next step of the journey. There's something appropriately hypnotic about providing value to draw people in, building reciprocity, and guiding them to the next logical step.

Is this manipulative? The truth is we're always influencing, so learn to do it ethically and respectfully. Use your powers for good! The strength of content marketing and lead generation is that you're learning to lead with value. You're improving people's experiences along the journey. Be sincere with your communication. Make it your goal for people to be better off than when they first found you. You can still produce raving fans and receive outstanding referrals even from people who haven't spent money on your services.

The benefit of producing media on a regular basis is that you're establishing a cycle of communication to launch your products while exponentially building more raving fans. The "know, like, and trust" momentum burns like an eternal flame. The small wins you create build a logical next step to go deeper into the relationship and become a paying customer.

This is your opportunity to brainstorm. What can you share with your potential audience? What experience can you provide? The simple answer? "Anything people can interact with." I've found the best result by mind-mapping headlines, titles, and specific themes. I only think about what platform is best for delivery once I have nailed the concept that needs to be shared. Your delivery mechanism could be an email, a paper flyer, an MP3 download, a series of videos, a live event, or almost anything else. The only limitations are your budget and imagination.

Modern technology has made "information-on-demand" an instant-gratification experience. I can turn on my phone and be in front of thousands of people in a matter of moments. Start producing content. Make a video. Start writing. Send an email. Draw something by hand and outsource it to someone else to design it into a marketing piece.

This "next step" doesn't have to be something involving a computer. Highlight your services with a free consultation either by phone or in person. Your time can be the "next step" along the lead generation journey to build value and rapport. My hypnosis business was originally built by offering a consultation to explore the process and talk about how it would work for them. The user experience of a free brief meeting established the rapport and expectation necessary to sign up for a program.

Ever walk through the food court of a shopping mall? Some restaurants' "next step" is a sample of their food. Ever attend an open house of a home for sale? The "next step" is to tour the home. Even a drug dealer's business model hinges on "the first taste is free," though I'd encourage you to be inspired by better metaphors!

It all comes back to starting and maintaining relationships. You hear a song that you like. You purchase the album. You watch clips of the singer on YouTube. You buy tickets to see the performer in concert. You buy t-shirts at the show. Maybe one day, you purchase the VIP meet-and-greet. Your journey began with a simple introduction.

Rapport will naturally be in place before you ask someone to make a purchase. I call this "The Willie Nelson Effect." I saw him in concert many years ago. At the end of the concert, he sat on the edge of the stage and signed hundreds of autographs. To overhear the conversations with fans, you'd think they already knew each other. These fans had been listening to his music for years, interacting in a dialogue with his songs, and the conversation naturally picked up in person for the first time.

Wouldn't you like your business to have that feeling? Build rapport so your clientele naturally feels a connection to you. Providing value builds a strong bond between you and your customer, eradicating the challenge of becoming a replaceable commodity. Deep rapport is in place before the sale is made.

Stories sell. Stories build value. Before a hypnosis client sees me to quit smoking, they watch a video on my website introducing a giant glass jar filled perhaps two-thirds with crushed up packs of cigarettes. I say, "Each pack of cigarettes tells a success story of someone just like you. Though I should mention why this jar is kind of empty. It's empty for a good reason." I produce a second glass jar overflowing with cigarettes, and I continue in the video, "It's because this one didn't have any room left. Please pick up the phone right now to talk about becoming a nonsmoker once and for all."

This strategy was effective given the surprise of the sight of so many thrown-out packs of cigarettes. The story drew in the audience to build rapport, and the call-to-action was well received. Thanks to the analytics of online marketing, I could track people who were watching the entire video and at what point they decided to call me.

For those who were on the fence in making a decision, I had an email opt-in series to receive further information on the process of quitting smoking. These two journeys into the same process had the same benefit. People were walking into my office with their cigarettes in hand ready to throw them away. I did not have to give the instruction, make the request, or even hint at a demand. They had conditioned themselves for the experience to be successful. By thinking in content marketing and lead generation principles, you create a better customer experience.

Nobody wants your newsletter. I know, I'm taking a risk in saying something that bold to you. You've read my book up until now, so I don't mean to offend. Allow me to explain myself. Imagine this:

"Hey! It's Tuesday! And because it's Tuesday, I'm sending you an email, because that's what I always do on Tuesdays!"

How exciting is that! It isn't. People have become immune to marketing messages. We see them all the time. In the words of Gary Vaynerchuk, we're all in the business of "day-trading attention."

Here's a better option. What if I knew you had an interest in improving your public speaking? Perhaps I had three specific conversational strategies you could implement immediately to become more ethically influential while reducing fears. Would you rather receive that or my Tuesday newsletter? Remember the goal is to provide an experience and create a personal win. Ride the momentum of this mini-success into the sale.

And thingify it. Make it a thing. Name it and make it something specific. "Public Speaking Tips" or "The 3-Step Influence System." Which would you rather have?

Make your offer stand out. Be memorable and specific. Avoid the challenge that confusion doesn't sell. Name your piece something short. Give it a subtitle to explain it. Want an example? You're reading it. The name of this book is a short title followed by a brief explainer subtitle. By the end of reading the title, you know what you're going to receive. That's likely why you picked up this book.

This strategy doesn't have to apply only to the first step of the lead generation journey. Brand and label all that you do to have a common language and become more memorable.

If I'm offering a class, it's never "click here to learn more." Instead, it's "click here to get the video test drive experience. Learn what it's like to take my class before you even take my class." I've shared this strategy with other speakers. As they branded their video welcome as a "backstage tour," their new client interactions grew.

Keep your focus on the relationship metaphor. Genuinely care about the people you're in a relationship with. I would insist you be authentic and maintain integrity with your customers. Business is noble when you're solving someone's problem. Create stronger relationships as you create a stronger business.

To tie it all together, the relationship continues even when they become your client. Through a principle of "onboarding," I created a "start here" video at the beginning of one of my flagship products. There were instructions to get more value throughout the program. I sold the "next step" even to people who had already paid me. The results were dramatic as people were getting even more value from the program. The side benefit was the product refund requests were virtually negated.

Put value at every step of your customer's journey. You will receive more value in return.

WORK SMART ACTION STEPS:

☞ Imagine yourself in the shoes of your potential client. What goals do they have? What challenges are they facing? What common questions are they asking? It's important to let the journey focus on their story even more than yours. Compile a list of their needs. This will become the roadmap for your content creation.

☞ Is there a part of your business that's struggling? Shift your perspective and ask where you are in the relationship with your audience? If you're trying to metaphorically consummate marriage before the first date, it's time to add a few more steps to your buying process. Enhance the relationship with your potential customer.

☞ Commit to a schedule of producing systems that will guide more people into your business. You can still continue to just sell your product directly. The benefit of adding lead generation to your strategy is a widening web to attract more people. People have different buying strategies, so you will appeal to a wider audience. Outsource the technology tasks that aren't an effective use of your time.

☞ Consider the people who are already paying you. What "next step" strategies can you implement to give them a greater experience? The more I've put value into my programs over the years, the more client referrals became the dominant force that drove the success of my business. Create systems to enhance customer satisfaction.

CREATIVE SOLUTIONS TO SOLVE PROBLEMS

Wayne Dyer once said, "If you change the way you look at things, the things you look at change."

Inside of you is the ability to WORK SMART in your creativity to address many of the challenges people face in their professional or even personal lives. How is it one conflict can stop a person in their tracks, yet the same conflict becomes an inspirational spark to someone else? The difference is in their thinking.

As much as I've shared the principle that "it's very rarely the platform, it's almost always the strategy," it's time we talk about mindset. My goal is to put specific action steps in your hands so you take action when things may seem stacked against you. This chapter will help you change your mindset.

Think of a current problem or challenge you may be facing. Is it business? Is it personal? For now, just label the issue. Before we explore the conflict in depth, simply acknowledge the block that might currently be there.

Start with the end in mind. Assume you've already resolved the issue and you're out there in this future result. At the end of this journey, what will you have learned? What skills will now be a part of you? What kind of growth will you have experienced?

Mentally zoom out the visual perspective of this scene, as if you could observe it all from start to finish. Realize there are so many different paths to get from the starting point to the end. Just as you could imagine floating out of this experience and observing it from a distance, you can imagine many more creative ways to resolve this conflict.

Here are some stories to illustrate the idea of "Creative Solutions to Dissolve Problems."

I speak to businesses and organizations about turning goals into actionable steps to create desired outcomes. Do you need your staff asking for referrals more consistently? Are there divisions in your company that are not yet working together as they should? Are there leadership themes that need reinforcement?

When I'm speaking with the executive team in advance of an event, I'm looking for the key solution-based statement that will become the theme of the presentation. If we don't yet have the specific conflict that needs to be resolved, the intended message will become diluted and unrealized.

At first, the response is too often generic and nonspecific. "We want our team to be motivated!" they request. I have to ask, "For what result?" You can throw all the darts you want, but, without the dartboard, they're not going to stick.

These business events often have a message to the staff that needs reinforcement. With the threat of downsizing, it's necessary to communicate that their jobs are safe and to highlight the business methods to move forward. "The robots are coming." Here's how we can better work together as a team to keep the human-to-human connection. They have a team of employees that need to be motivated to perform as leaders.

Did you see the movie *Office Space*? It's a parody about a business that hung a banner reading, "Is this good for the company?" Modern CEOs and administrative teams know you need something creative to lock in the right message. I start my conversation with the executive team with a "needs analysis" to customize the program I'm going to present to the staff. The presentation features the core message of the company, shares specific mental strategies to internalize goals, plus humorous hypnotic experiences to highlight solutions in a memorable way.

The formula is "show," rather than "tell." Rather than LECTURE people about their problems, or simply issue a memo with the organization's new mission statement, the method is to generate a creative solution to show how to move forward. Actions speak louder than words.

As I spoke to schools, the creative solution to "show" people working together and becoming good community members was absorbed faster than simply lecturing to the students. They're already being bombarded with messages to "Do this" or "Don't do that." By thinking outside the box on how the message is delivered, we potentially hedge off major issues later when they become adults.

These were examples of organizations finding a creative way to demonstrate a necessary goal. You can do this to shift your thinking about your own perceived personal conflicts.

An executive shared with me that he felt self-conscious and anxious in social environments at work. The stress and fear he experienced would turn his face into an incredible shade of red, like a tomato, thanks to his Irish complexion. If he was nervous, it was obvious to everyone around. We could have spent our time focusing on how to cope with the problem. Instead, the focus was on a creative solution. In our coaching session, we uncovered the source of this fear was his concern that he wouldn't remember people's names. If a name slipped his mind, his body responded with fear and increased blood-flow to his face.

He smiled with delight as he hypothesized, "What if I became world-class at remembering names?" Rather than shining the personal change spotlight on the secondary issue of the fear, we focused his unconscious efforts on becoming a better listener, being in the moment with people, and installing important information in his memory. In addition to generating a creative solution to dissolve a problem, he turned a weakness into a strength!

I was inspired by his story as he rapidly improved. The blushing was no longer an issue, and he was more visible and influential at work. Want to know his secret to remembering names? He listened. He wasn't focused on what he was going to say next. He wasn't running his own mental programs. He was mindfully in the moment and genuinely cared to know the person. He attached genuine emotion to meeting new people as they would help advance his career, build a better community, and improve the lives of his family. "When I'm meeting someone new, they're the most important person in the world to me at that moment," he said. There was no need for memory tricks. The social anxiety and blushing issue rapidly resolved itself.

The best problems in life are the ones we create ourselves. I helped the vice president of a company overcome his fear of public speaking. I helped him become more influential and effective in his speaking, so his unconscious mind had no reason to hold onto an unnecessary fear. He wanted to overcome the speaking issue to become more visible at work and be considered for future promotions.

"I've got a brand-new problem, Jason!" he excitedly shared when he a called me a year later. The speaking challenge had been long resolved, and he was successful in getting a massive promotion. The new position, however, came with a new problem. He had to manage a team of people who did great work together but did not get along. He laughed as he told me that even his three teenage sons weren't as unruly as his staff. "You don't have to like each other, you just have to work together," he told them at work. He explained that he could handle the stress while on the job. "Hey, it's worth an extra $60,000 a year to have to deal with this," he joked. By comparison, a part of the creative solution to dissolve his problem was to appreciate it was a more manageable challenge than the one he originally had. We worked to reduce his stress and leave the challenges of the day at work where they belonged.

A hypnosis client of mine released the weight and frustration of losing and gaining back the same 20 pounds over and over. He was yo-yo dieting. When success seemed imminent, he would backslide in his momentum and gain the weight back. He knew it was a simple formula to adjust his eating and exercise habits. There was no secret to burning away the excess fat on his body. Unfortunately, some life event would pop up, he'd lose momentum, and suddenly realize he had gained the weight back.

What was his creative solution? He now focused on becoming fit rather than losing fat. He focused on the new creative solution rather than the problem. The result? He easily achieved a lean body fat percentage while gaining a significant amount of muscle mass. Success is contagious. His story helped inspire me to get into strength training.

My wife and I had the issue that our children would sometimes eat everything on their plates other than the vegetables. It's not that my children are picky eaters. They can be rather adventurous at times trying new foods. The creative solution was to tell them we were going to start doing something fancy with our meals. The nicer restaurants bring your meal out in courses! The first course would be the vegetables, then they'd bring out something new. We'd highlight this feature if we were dining out with them. Rather than get into an argument and throw logic at them on the importance of good nutrition, it was a perceived treat that we were eating in a fancy way.

Let's go back to my story of opening my business and signing the big scary lease. Rather than focus my attention on "How am I going to afford this?" I shifted to "What business opportunities can I create so the expense is no longer a concern?"

Where can you put your attention now? I'm not suggesting you play the game of ignoring a conflict. Unattended problems may sometimes get worse.

Bring your thoughts back to the conflict you identified at the beginning of this chapter. Here's a creative way to think about it. You're already a different person than you were when you started reading this chapter. Your body is an incredible physiological system that is always generating new cells to replace the ones that die off at an automated pace, so you don't have to worry about it. Your skin is different. Your organs are different. Your mind is different. Even in the subtlest ways, the physical body you're in now is already different than it was moments ago. You're always in a stage of physical change. Your mind is always adapting to new ideas and situations.

Just because something was one way before is no reason it has to be that way now. What creative solution are you going to focus on now?

WORK SMART ACTION STEPS:

☞ Compile a list of possible roadblocks that might be holding back your personal or business success. The action of simply writing them down may be transformational for you. The magic of disassociation happens when you can view the conflicts on paper rather than just perceived thoughts in your mind. A client of mine was struggling with her productivity due to the extreme fatigue she was facing. She burst out laughing as she wrote down the sentence, "I can't get to bed at a reasonable time." The idea that this skill wasn't within her abilities became ridiculous to her. She easily created the ritual of giving herself a specific bedtime.

☞ I'm serious about what I'm about to suggest to you. Based on your list of conflicts, brainstorm for a few minutes the most ridiculous strategies or mindsets to observe the situation differently. Exercise creativity here without editing. Know that throwing out the "bad ideas" will help you arrive at the good ones. Inside one of those silly ideas may be something brilliant that changes your life.

☞ Reach out for help. The journey of an entrepreneur doesn't have to be a solo adventure. Talk the situation through with a friend. Buy a training program to learn better solutions. Hire someone to help you. Do the self-hypnosis you'll learn later in this book. It comes from a position of strength to accept there's something you can't yet do on your own. The most important word of the previous sentence was the word "yet." You've got this.

BE HYPNOTIC

How can a hypnotist help you grow your business? Through the streams of my live sessions and events, plus my digital-access programs, I've hypnotized more than 250,000 people. I've used the skills of rapport and modeling to track what makes people successful. I've asked athletes, politicians, actors, entrepreneurs, and CEOs from all walks of life: "What's the one thing that makes you the most successful?" The strategies that I've unpacked from studying these people has helped me easily triple the size of my business and go on to build a million-dollar brand.

You're about to learn that hypnosis doesn't have to be just a process. It doesn't just have to be the experience of coming to my office or flying me to your place of business to work with you and your team. Of course, I'd love to meet you. I'm easy to track down!

You're about to learn that hypnosis can become a state of mind. It can become a philosophy. It can become a way of looking differently at the world around you. It can become a mindset I like to call "Hypnotic Tenacity."

That mindset in which you are absolutely certain you're going to make something happen.

Allow me to share with you how you can "Be Hypnotic."

But first, let me tell you the story of a man who calls me up and explains that he's stuck. His professional tone informs me that there's a challenge in his business. He's lost his motivation to scale up his company in recent years. He has several big-picture ideas, but he's caught in analysis paralysis. He has "too many good ideas," so where should he start?

We meet for a series of private sessions, and, suddenly, things are different. It's like a firecracker's fuse is ignited. He's completing tasks on time. He's motivated to complete jobs. He's easily knocking things off his to-do list.

It's now the sixth time we've met, and he's on a roll. In the theme of "Creative Solutions," we're no longer discussing his previously perceived problem. All of our processes are focused on solutions. The process is working better than he imagined it would.

The rapport of our working relationship is running deep, so I decide to become a little confrontational. I ask a question that he has been skirting around since our initial phone call. Something obvious has been left out of all our discussions. "You realize I have no idea what you do for a living, don't you?" Up until this moment, when he's spoken about his fears and anxious feelings, he has been vividly descriptive. If I've asked what specific tasks he does in his daily work, he has generically branded everything as "running my business."

We've spent hours in the room together releasing some serious conflicts he had held onto for years. It's painfully obvious I still don't know what line of work he's in. In response, he simply smiled and said, "Isn't that interesting?" To this day, I still have no clue what line of work he was in. At least he promised it was legal.

This story is the perfect transition to officially introduce hypnosis. I first encountered hypnosis when a hypnotist did a presentation at my college. That sparked a never-ending quest of learning all that I could about the power of the mind.

I cobbled together a demonstration of hypnosis, which I would do for friends. At one of my first presentations, my wife, who I was only dating at the time, expressed, "That was good. However, you should work on the expression on your face that telegraphs, 'Wow, it's actually working!'" I was inspired to seek out a community, and I became certified by the major hypnosis organizations around the world.

And yes, I've heard the joke many times before: "Did you hypnotize your wife to fall in love with you?" No. Though our son was a HypnoBirthing baby, as she naturally gave birth without any pain medication!

I began my career with motivational programs for schools and colleges, which has now evolved into my corporate presentations. By mixing education and audience participation, we can deliver a positive message in an unforgettable way.

I soon opened Virginia Hypnosis, one of the leading hypnotherapy centers in the United States. I continue to work with dozens of clients on a regular basis for the goals of quitting smoking, motivating new behaviors, and overcoming fears. Many of my clients are executives or athletes seeking high-level mental coaching.

Don't let the word hypnosis scare you. As I work with top performers in these industries, I often find that some of the most successful people out there are already hypnotizing themselves. They just don't call it hypnosis. They call it creative visualization. They call it getting into the right frame of mind or getting in the zone. Thanks to Dave Elman, an early twentieth-century pioneer of the profession, hypnosis is most often defined as the "bypassing of the critical faculties of the conscious mind and the acceptance of positive selective thinking in the subconscious mind."

That's a lot of technical jargon. Let's break it down. The "bypassing of the critical faculties" refers to an automatic response in spite of conscious awareness. We do this on our own every single day. You could be driving in your car thinking of everything other than driving your car. You still end up where you would like to go. You could be watching a movie. You know everything up there is fiction. It's all made up. The actors are wearing costumes and playing make-believe. We know it's all fake, but we still get swept up in the story.

How does this apply to personal change? Think about the problems a person may be facing as they come into my hypnosis office.

It's no secret that cigarettes are unhealthy and are slowly killing people. Yet some people are buying them by the carton and smoking a full pack every day. They're bypassing conscious knowledge to follow an unconscious habit.

It's a natural part of life to experience stress, frustration, or even boredom. Yet there are some people out there who feel this emotional reaction; they know the feeling has nothing to do with food, and they're eating as a subconscious distraction. They don't consciously think, "This food is going to make me happier!" They know it's only a temporary distraction, yet many people fall into this emotional eating trap.

Fears work the same way. Some people are afraid of flying. Statistically, you are safer in the air than you were driving to the airport! Consider the most common fear: public speaking. I've had executives in my office whose names were plastered on the outside of tall buildings and printed on the payroll checks of all their employees. In spite of their obvious authority, they would shake and stammer while speaking to their team.

These are all examples of people naturally bypassing conscious awareness. Through the patterns of hypnotic language and utilizing hypnotic phenomenon, I'm helping that person facilitate a change to integrate the knowledge they already have. Take those things you've already been saying to yourself, and this time, let's make them actually stick!

A man was in my office several years ago with the goal of quitting his two-pack-a-day cigarette smoking habit. We're having a friendly conversation about his intended goals. His tone suddenly shifts. "You're just going to persuade me," he accuses. "Of course I am," I reply. "I'm going to persuade you to do those things you've already decided to do. You just haven't yet been able to do them on your own. Sounds like a good use of your time and money, doesn't it?" He laughed. I'm happy to report he's still a nonsmoker many years later.

Hypnosis is in a renaissance of acceptance and understanding around the world. There are news stories released on a daily basis of people making positive breakthroughs in their lives. It's no longer in the category of deciding whether or not someone "believes" or "doesn't believe" in the process. There are more than 280,000 studies to be read on Google Scholar speaking of its efficacy. Studies in neuroscience now suggest amazing evidence as to what regions of the brain are activating in the process. From an evolutionary psychological perspective, it's a state of mind that has been around ever since there were people. We've only labeled it with the word "hypnosis" in the last 150 years.

It's a skill that people can learn to use to help others or even themselves. I have a passion for sharing it with others. I've trained and certified hundreds of students around the world to master the skills of hypnosis and to launch their own businesses helping private clients. I've received awards for being a leading educator and innovator in our community of hypnotists.

Hypnosis is a state of accelerated learning. The mind can rapidly integrate new beliefs and new understandings to fast-track personal change. Some people would say it takes 30 days to install a new behavior. I would say those people might not be using the best of methods.

The stories and themes I've shared so far are how my local business flourished during my start-up and scale up phases. Remember the vaudeville sentiment I previously shared: "The amateur changes their act and the professional changes their audience." The truth is, it's not just one or the other. As you take your message to a larger community, it must adapt to fit the desires of the new audience and the changing medium. I pivoted the skills I was using in my private office, classroom, and speaking engagements to a global audience with a new project carrying a name that might sound familiar.

Work Smart Hypnosis.

The hub of that business is "The Work Smart Hypnosis Podcast with Jason Linett." It's an industry-specific program broadcasting to the micro-niche of hypnotists around the world. This media project became the platform for my online training programs which are viewed internationally. I have thousands of hours of content online and, at any moment in time, someone, somewhere in the world, is listening to me or watching me. My business is running even while I'm speaking on stage, working with a private client, or spending time with my wife and kids. The podcasts and training programs were my asset that leveraged invitations to travel the world teaching what I do. The visibility of live training programs and private services increased as I continued to launch several digital-access membership programs.

Even though my businesses were given titles such as "Virginia Hypnosis" or "Work Smart Hypnosis," I became the brand. People were buying the "Jason Linett" brand. As soon as I embraced the positioning of my own identity, the combined revenue over a few years totaled more than a million dollars. The "Willie

Nelson Effect" I introduced in the lead generation chapter became my life. I would attend a convention of new people, and they already knew me. My live training events and private sessions would begin as if continuing a conversation we'd been having for years.

WORK SMART became a command statement. Work with intention, focus, and purpose. Apple inspired their computer users to "think different." By shifting my thinking to WORK SMART and think differently, I discovered a correlation that all people in business need to embrace.

The way you are here is the way you are everywhere else. The amateur changes their act, and the professional changes their audience.

I now share the concepts of leveraging assets, building rituals, and shifting your perceptual position in the business world. I teach specific mental strategies to take goals out of your mind and off your paper, and, instead, into your reality. The attendees of my presentations can immediately implement these methods to enhance their business. As it is my expertise, self-hypnosis is the primary strategy I share to help people change the way they think.

My journey is one of leveraging each experience to the next one, to the next one, and, again, to the next one. My mission with this book is for you to live your entrepreneurial dream. Create something incredible. The real message of this book? If I can do these things in a profession where I have to spend time dispelling the myths and misconceptions of hypnosis, you've got it easier than I did. You can create your success even faster and more easily. In your line of work, hopefully, you don't have to explain to people that you're not going to make them cluck like a chicken. I'd honestly tell you I've never even seen any hypnotist ask someone to do that! Before my work can even begin, I have to inoculate against the fears people hold about hypnosis. You're likely in a much more normal profession than I am!

You might be a real estate agent. You might be a plumber or a contractor. You could be a photographer. You don't have to overcome the barriers I have to achieve success. If I was able to build several six-figure businesses in my unique category of work. Your opportunity is even greater. Without the challenge of helping people overcome fears, misconceptions, and myths, you can get straight to work.

Please model my story and model the story of your potential clients. What's holding you back? What's holding them back? The narrative you build that bridges the two stories may build your own million-dollar brand.

From my experiences, I've learned that hypnosis doesn't just have to be a formal process. It can become a philosophy. Step into the result you're ready to create and make it happen with tenacity. Become highly suggestible to your experiences as you learn along the way. A principle in hypnotic work is that "there is no failure, there is only feedback."

It's not just the simple suggestion to "fake it until you make it." From my previous career working with actors, I learned a principle of improvisational acting is "act as if." Focus your strategies and efforts on WHEN they will work for you, rather than IF. Talk about your goals as if you've already achieved them. Embrace the journey this becomes, like the classic video game reference I previously shared. Be honest about where you are in the process and eliminate the strategies that aren't working.

Later in this book, I'm going to share with you a simple and direct self-hypnosis strategy I've taught to thousands of people. But first, I'm going to give you a bonus. Here's self-hypnosis in just one sentence:

"Talk about what you want, rather than what you don't want."

In hypnosis, we make statements for positive change called hypnotic suggestions. The formula to deliver a hypnotic suggestion is simple. It's an action followed by a result. It's a cause followed by an effect.

Imagine that a person is ready to launch their business, yet they're procrastinating. Through conversational and formal hypnotic methods, we get their mind working as if they were already productive.

Rather than focus on the problem of procrastinating, they step into the creative solution of connecting their mind to a reality as if they were already working and already being successful. "Look into the future and remember how well you will have done" is a phrase that frames the process. Retrain the mental automatic response to step into that change as if that's what you've always been doing. Rather than "fake it until you make it," perhaps consider it as "train the neurology."

Act as if. Step into that reality as if you've already achieved it. Allow your old negative thinking to atrophy and let this new pattern of thought grow stronger and become the upgraded representation within the mind.

A hypnotic suggestion is an action followed by a result.

As you start creating content to better inform your clients, you develop a greater understanding of the importance of your work. As you start receiving positive feedback from your existing clients, you realize there's a greater need for your service worldwide. As you discover the greater opportunities to grow your business, you serve a greater good in the world around you. As you speak about what you do and feel your own voice resonating in the chambers of your body, you feel an incredibly genuine confidence growing each and every day.

Set your life in motion. It's not just about making an affirmation of something you want. It's about putting momentum into your life. One of the words inside of "attraction" is "action." Put action into your words to set your goals in motion. Re-read the previous paragraph. I was using hypnotic language patterns throughout the entire sequence. As you do this, notice that. As you notice that, you find it is easier to do this. Let your actions become the hypnotic suggestion and a catalyst for change.

Get started right away. Talk about what you want, rather than about what you don't want. It's the classic law of concentrated attention. Set your mind toward the goal. Give yourself permission to acknowledge what you're good at. It's time for a self-induced pat on the back. Embrace your strengths and put them to use.

I had the advantage of growing up in a family where everyone was an entrepreneur. There was never an expectation for me to go into the family business. I went to college following one path and decided to completely abandon that industry to run off and become a hypnotist. The metaphorical equivalent would have been to run off and join the circus. Though with my brief hobby of doing magic tricks, the circus may have been a definite possibility.

I encourage you to "Be Hypnotic." Set goals and go after them. Rather than play the game of "What if," instead, focus on "What will I do about it." Act with certainty and tenacity. If I decide I'm going to do something, I'm determined to make it happen. There's a quote from Lorne Michaels, the creator and producer of Saturday Night Live: "Whether we're ready or not, the show goes live at 11:30."

This mindset can change your world. You can do hypnosis, or you can "Be Hypnotic." Make a mental decision to step into a result as if you have already achieved it. Change the pictures in your mind and focus yourself on being a person of action. Open yourself to much greater opportunities. Take ownership of your own state of mind, your communication with others, and even with yourself. Open yourself up to greater flexibility and possibility for growth.

Things will change. Many companies pivot their focus as they grow and listen to their consumers. A computer manufacturer started selling music. An online bookstore is now running your local grocery store. An actor moved into politics. I watched a funny show on stage in college that transmuted into speaking to businesses about turning goals into realities and coaching private clients.

Transmute. That's a word you don't often hear these days. Go back and read *Think and Grow Rich* by Napoleon Hill for a classic lesson on lifestyle design.

What's that big goal of yours? Take a moment to "Be Hypnotic" as you think about what it would be like to have already reached it. Turn up that burning desire to make it happen. Shift it from a "should" to a "must." Create your own mental state of "Hypnotic Tenacity." Identify a goal, put action to it, and find creative solutions to dissolve the problems.

I recently achieved the goal of speaking to my biggest audience ever. Back to Kevin Pollak: "If you're not creating, you're waiting." Rather than just hoping I could speak on this platform, I took massive action. I hired a team of research analysts to study the industry I wished to speak to. They helped me craft the right message to send to the right people. The speaking opportunity was soon mine, and the event was a success. More importantly, I leveraged this opportunity into the higher positioning necessary to grow in a new market.

Continue to pivot your success in the way that aligns with your personal goals. Open up your full conscious awareness to all the possibilities that are there. Lock onto the tenacity of "I am going to make this work."

There's a hypnotic word I've held back from explaining until now.

Trance.

My definition of trance is very simple. It's when your internal representations carry more importance than external representations. Your inner experience becomes paramount over the external reality. Despite conscious logic, the unconscious mind can hold onto a false perception to protect you. A person flying might be creating an internal trance of fear. The public speaker may be shaking as he creates the internal trance of nervousness.

This is why I often say that I'm not really hypnotizing people to produce a change. Instead, we're de-hypnotizing the unnecessary self-limiting beliefs and blocks that were holding you back up until now. The truth is, if you can create one trance, you can create another. Create the "working productively" trance. Create the "releasing negativity to those things I cannot control" trance. Step into the "live in the present moment" trance.

Change the "every reason I can't do this" trance into an "it's the right time" trance. Draw a straight line from here to where you'd like to be. Decide that it's going to be easy. Decide that it's going be fun.

WORK SMART and BE HYPNOTIC.

WORK SMART ACTION STEPS:

☞ Make time for yourself. Revisit the goals you've mapped out in the earlier action steps of this book. Enhance them. Make them bigger. Define a timeframe in which you're going to make that happen. You might be surprised that a map to get there is clearer now than it ever was before.

☞ I met a pilot who explained that the flight-plan for an airline is perfect on paper. Yet, as soon as he leaves the gate at the airport, they constantly have to make modifications for other planes, weather, and whatever other conditions may be present. However, he always lands the plane. Embrace that you will need to make modifications and have some real learning experiences along your business journey. Look for meaning in every moment to enhance your learning and entrepreneurial strength.

☞ Commit now to make use of the self-hypnosis strategy taught later in this book. It takes less than a minute, and, through simple repetition, you can focus your mind toward better actions and outcomes.

KEEP BALANCE

What if the lesson of a nervous actor could change the way you think about your business? What if the secret to becoming a better person involved injecting an appropriate dash of greed in your life? Imagine what could happen if you decided right now is the best time to take serious action growing your business.

I want you to have an incredible business. I want the work you do to inspire the lives of others. My real message to you is this: I want you to have a life of your own.

We've now built the foundation to WORK SMART in your business. It's time, now, to create balance in your life. Together, we're going to explore strategies to avoid burnout, build amazing relationships with loved ones, and discover the reasons beyond money to have your own business.

You picked up and are reading a book with the title *WORK SMART BUSINESS*. I can assume there is something you hope to achieve by reading this book. This might be your first business book. You may have already read through the classics. In *The E-Myth Revisited*, Michael Gerber informed you that you were working too much IN your business rather than ON your business. In *Think and Grow Rich*, Napoleon Hill helped you ignite a "burning desire" to change your life. I sincerely thank you for joining me. Our journey together is really just beginning. I'd like you to enjoy your WORK. I want you to be SMART about how you go from start-up to scale up. I want your BUSINESS to be something that makes the world a better place for yourself and for all of us.

Let's get personal. To WORK SMART means to have a life outside of your business. It's important to step away from your work. One part of life balances out the other. Strive to create the appropriate balance between life and work so you don't burn out. Make time for friends, family, loved ones, even for vacations.

I burned out hard while working in theatrical production management. I was behind the scenes organizing million-dollar-budget shows with dozens of actors and musicians. Sometimes, children and animals on stage were thrown into the mix. Then add a bunch of designers, moving scenery, union contracts, Microsoft Excel spreadsheets, and tons of time spent in the dark. Plus, for some reason, the company I worked at had a knack for picking plays where the backstage crew had to cook a full English breakfast for the actors to eat on stage, because that's what the play called for. My level of burnout was simply remarkable.

I was on track to be promoted to what had originally been my perceived "dream job." The Christmas holidays were rapidly approaching, and we found ourselves working until midnight. I wanted to be at home with my family. I was there alongside one of my mentors who commented, "You work like this because you love the art. That's why you give your life to it."

Something clicked at that moment. It was never the same after that. Hypnosis had been a hobby up until this point. Even just doing the occasional program for schools and seeing occasional clients, I was actually earning more from my part-time passion than my full-time career. It turns out that nonprofit arts are nonprofit for almost everybody involved!

It all happened sooner than I expected. The "dream job" offer was presented, and it felt like getting punched in the stomach. I could not spend my life like this anymore. I politely declined the offer, walked away, went all-in on the life of the entrepreneur, and I haven't looked back.

Just because you're good at something doesn't mean you have to do it for the rest of your life.

This is the first time I've shared my story in such detail. I'm still friends with many of the people I worked with in those days and, if I could go back in time, I wouldn't change a thing. The lessons of balancing creative personalities prepared me for a career working with people for personal change. I'd credit most of my ability to design business systems to the experience coordinating the backstage operations of a big-budget production. My time management skills were sharpened to near-perfection by having to know the exact details and timing of every actor's backstage costume changes and entrances. Backstage theater technicians naturally become a jack of all trades. This flexibility gave me tenacious energy to keep learning how to do new things. The artistic passion didn't have to die, it just had to pivot. I can enjoy sitting in the audience of a good show. I don't have to be the one backstage!

I share my origin story because some of you may just be at the dreaming stage of the entrepreneurial journey. If it's not yet the time for you to take the leap, my advice is to start incubating. I spent my final weeks of the theater job only working a "production" schedule rather than "rehearsal." A rehearsal schedule is basically a nine-to-five job. Production involves the running of the show, which means you're there from about 5pm to midnight. It's a rough schedule as you have no social life, but it was the perfect scenario as I was building my websites, designing my client programs, booking more speaking opportunities, and preparing to transition immediately upon my exit. Design your exit strategy to become the perfect entrance to the next part of your entrepreneurial story.

This reminds me of a story. Whether you have experience in theater or not you've likely been told, when giving a presentation make sure the audience can see your face. Whether you're thinking back to elementary school or even a boardroom meeting, you're told to stand so people can see your face.

I was sitting behind a folding table in a rehearsal hall when an actor in his early twenties was directed to stand with his back facing the audience. This clearly caused him stress. Maybe it hurt his feelings that the audience wouldn't see his smiling face. Maybe there was a concern as to what his friends and family would say? They were going to travel a long distance to see his performance, just to see the back of his head. Here he was at the start of his career, tens of thousands of dollars in student loan debt, and his professional career would begin with his back to the audience.

He was not pleased, but he was polite. Like a good actor, he was also creative. "What if I stood over here?" he asked the director. He was told no. "What if I'm helping with the table," he said, as he tried to become a part of the play's action.

The director walked over to him and explained: "I'm giving you a gift. You have the most important line of the play in a few moments. By having your back to the audience, we'll have you turn and face the audience just before you say that line. This will guarantee everyone in the audience will be looking directly at you. By turning around, you're making another entrance. Every set of eyes in the room will be looking at you. This way they will all hear you. I'm allowing you to make a new entrance when you're already on stage."

Clearly, this appealed to the ego of the young man. The funny thing is that he then spent the rest of the rehearsal process trying to fight for more opportunities to turn his back to the audience.

I come back to this story often as it illustrates the value of stepping away. It allows you to make another introduction. The brain is like a muscle. Give it the opportunity to release focus and shift attention to other things. Your mind can come back with greater intent.

Do you like your job? Do you hate your job? Either way, step away from it. Even if it's just for a weekend or a few hours. Even when things seem at their absolute best. Step away to release stress. Give yourself a rest to come back with greater focus.

I have to assume that you're driven by a specific passion. If not, perhaps it's time to review your goals and objectives. If you're not congruent with your goals, you're likely to fizzle out or burn out. Passion is that initial spark that drives us to gather the skills, invest the time, and become energized to make something happen.

You are the director of your own life. Sometimes you may be on other people's schedules and job requirements. You still have a say in how you spend your life. Take the steps necessary to either find or make the balance in your life.

Take better care of yourself. Give yourself permission to be respectfully greedy with your time. Make time to be with family and friends. Make time to exercise and eat right. Have a life outside of work.

Life isn't just about money. Time is one of those things that if you don't spend it wisely, you don't get to enjoy the benefits of it in the future. Leverage your schedule to have full control of your time. You'll be better able to enjoy your finances, your family, and even your own health.

When I made my theatrical exit and entrepreneurial entrance, I was hungry. I stood in an empty office having signed a big lease with the conviction that there wasn't an option to fail. I was going to make it work. I positioned myself without an exit strategy. I took on every opportunity I could find. If a client needed an 8:30am appointment, I scheduled it at that time. If they needed 9:00pm in the evening, I arranged my schedule to accommodate their needs.

I was spending all my time at the office working with a ton of clients. Business was rapidly growing. In spite of the financial success, I lost track of relationships with friends, and I gained about twenty pounds. I was running my business life like a horse with blinders.

That was before I had children. My wife was commuting long hours for a job at the time, so even though our schedules matched up, something had to change. I had to take control of my time. I had to balance it out.

I shifted my schedule to lock in specific office hours. Rather than "whenever you want," I decided that I would only see four people a day. The schedule became a rigid 10am, 12pm, 2pm, or 4pm option. If someone told me that 3:30 worked best for them, I'd offer my 4pm timeslot. If they asked about weekends or evening appointments, I reiterated my weekday business hours. My initial fear was that doing this would push my clients away. I saw a completely opposite reaction. Many more people were now booking with me. If at first glance my hours were not ideal, they would call me back to update that they had shifted their schedules to accommodate me! Remember, there's no such thing as finding the time. There's making the time. They shifted their thinking to realize the importance of achieving their goal and made the time to work specifically with me. Perhaps balance is viral? As I created balance in my life, they created it in theirs.

Pay yourself first with your time. Pay yourself first with your health. Health is one of those things that if we don't care for it now, we don't get to enjoy it as much in the future. I can draw a direct correlation between the quality of my family life and my business and the quality of my health. Everything in life improved when I changed my eating habits, eliminated alcohol from my life, and made going to the gym a ritual. I easily tripled my income while I made these changes in my life.

There's no such thing as finding the time. Finding the time is a game we invented to convince ourselves that there are things we're too busy to do. If you're stuck in the "finding the time" game, perhaps it's time to turn up that burning desire to make something happen. Or maybe it's not really your burning desire. Let your own family life, personal life, and health also be a burning desire.

Create an incredible business so you can step away from it. Go out with friends. Be there at your kids' school when they have special events. Take a vacation. Let the business brain have a break. Pay yourself first. Enjoy this gift of being alive.

I stopped working on holidays. If my kids are off from school on a Monday because it's a federal holiday, I also take the day off. When we're on vacation, the business calls go either to voicemail or an assistant. Let home be home and let work be work.

In my business, I often ask myself the question of "What is this going to earn me?" rather than "What is this going to cost me?" When my primary video camera died, it was annoying. I had purchased that camera for about $1500 many years ago. It was a reliable machine for at least five years. I had generated hundreds of thousands of dollars with that camera. It didn't take much to justify spending $3,000 on the next camera; I knew the value it would provide me.

Think this way with your personal life. In spite of the extended "pay yourself first" metaphor from earlier in this chapter, sometimes spending a little money goes a long way. It would take me an entire day to clean my house. Badly. We often pay someone else to come and do it right and in less time. This allows us more meaningful time with our kids or perhaps a night out.

Put down your phone. Engage in conversation. Really experience the world around you. Don't become a slave to your business by working on holidays, scheduling meetings at odd hours, and exiting the dinner table with your family to take a business call. I've developed a greater rapport with my clients by politely telling them I'm not available until a certain time because I'm with my family.

Just like the young actor, this allows you to make a grand entrance. Move back into the business mode with sharper focus and a greater appreciation of the passion that fuels your efforts. You'll be more refreshed. Your production at work will be greater.

Will business still be on your mind? There will always be passing thoughts. The simple strategy of having an ongoing to-do list simply in the Notes app of my phone allows me to briefly jot down these ideas. Just like financial savings, making a brief note is like making a small investment that will pay a massive dividend later.

The little things in life add up. Make your bed. Clean out your car. Do something good for your health. Donate your time to a good cause. Spend your time enjoying the life you've built rather than just working through life. Let your external balance become your internal balance. Sounds like a good trance state, doesn't it?

Pay yourself first with your time.

WORK SMART ACTION STEPS:

☞ The next section of this book contains tested strategies to take the ten WORK SMART principles you've learned and turn them into realities. Before you start implementing the strategies, open your calendar and make time for yourself. Reach out to a friend, go to a concert, or perhaps take your kids outside to play with them.

☞ Go for a walk, let your mind rest, and come back ready to make your next entrepreneurial entrance.

WORK SMART STRATEGIES

THE WORK SMART BUSINESS SYSTEM

You've learned about the concept of building systems to run your business. I'm going to share my favorite system for scaling up my business with you.

Consider these two options for generating new business:

Option #1: You invest a lot of time, energy, and money into a new venture. Several weeks or months are spent crafting the perfect product and marketing materials to inspire people to join you. Time passes, and now your product is ready to launch. You finally put it out to the world, and you receive a surprising reaction.

Nothing. Nobody wants it. Assuming your promotional efforts were effective, perhaps you failed to properly market test to see if people actually wanted what you had to offer.

Option #2: You schedule a class you'd like to teach about six months from now. You could host the event in your own office space, though you've called around to local conference centers to screen availability should the attendance grow larger than expected. People start to respond to your offer as they're now signing up for your event. Your agenda for the course begins to change as the registrants explain their motivation in signing up for your course. The event is a success in your own space, and the profit is high considering the low expense.

Here's another option #2. Let's stick with the theme of an event. You schedule a specific "start-up" course as a tripwire for people to experience your service. Somehow your promotion draws a different quality of student than you expected. Rather than inexperienced newbies, you attract people with significant experience. Your starter class morphs into a mastermind group. Perhaps some of these people hire you for your services or buy your products.

And yet another option #2. Your event is getting an incredible response. You book the conference center at the point of threshold as you're going to have three times the amount of people in the audience than you had expected.

The best problems in life are the ones we invent ourselves.

It would be a shame to spend hundreds of hours crafting a massive online educational course to then discover it's something no one needs. This WORK SMART BUSINESS SYSTEM allows you to launch incredible projects in a flexible way to minimize risk. Rather than pour all your efforts into the big product, start with something small. Produce a one-hour training video teaching one key concept. Test the market by selling just this video. Based on the response, you will discover if people really have a need for it.

When in doubt, ask! You will have created a community of people who have bought your single-hour video product. Make contact with them by sending emails, calling them, or create an online survey to discover their greatest needs. Listen to their concerns, and create your big product based on their feedback. You will have already harnessed the power of community. These people will likely be first in line when the bigger system launches.

The WORK SMART BUSINESS SYSTEM is a principle that maximizes productivity and minimizes effort. Start small, listen for feedback, and meet a specific need. It's just like a relationship. Go out on a few metaphorical "dates" with your audience to make sure things are a match. This strategy drives you to be flexible.

Listen to your audience and build the product that they want. I'm suggesting this system from the assumption that you really do have a product or service that people need. However, take note that I'm suggesting you build the product your audience wants.

Their wants and needs are different. Making the offer based on their want will grab their attention and likely result in closed business. Once inside the product, you should absolutely deliver what they're looking for. This provides the opportunity to leverage the interaction into delivering what they need. This system positions you for the ultimate under-promise over-deliver outcome.

The WORK SMART BUSINESS SYSTEM saves you time and money. In the previous example of a successful event, you're only scaling up your expenses as the event scales up. For the successful product example, you're only investing the time and money to build it based on the feedback of people who have already identified themselves as your ideal buyers.

Start with what's appropriate for your given time and budget. My first hypnosis office was a professional space, but I did not break my budget before the money was rolling in. I put my time, energy, and money toward marketing and promotion, and that's how I built the business I have today.

WORK SMART ACTION STEPS:

☞ Start with the end in mind. What big goal would you like to achieve? Break it down into smaller, reasonable chunks. Choose a much easier entry point for your market and explore this smaller project to test for your audience's wants and needs.

☞ Keep in mind the difference between their wants and their needs. Model the language you hear from your potential clients. You will discover the perfect entry point in this market. Think small to earn big.

REFRAMING

As a hypnotist, I help people change their minds. This often starts by helping people change their words. It's a small conscious exercise that may deliver a big unconscious change. Put a different name or alternate set of words on something, and the perspective changes. Shifting perspective words can often make the biggest difference. What happens when "my fear" becomes "that issue" you used to deal with?

I'm going to share with you some examples of what's called "Reframing" in this chapter. Even though some of the concepts are business related, while others are personal, you may exercise creativity to apply them to any part of your life.

A picture is worth a thousand words. Put a beautiful painting on the wall in an ornate frame in a posh museum. We might call it a masterpiece. Stick the picture in an ugly, broken, dirty frame, and we might just give it another word? Garbage.

The formula for reframing is based on a simple concept. The structure of language is something that people had to invent over time. Through advances in science, the structure of the brain is something we're learning more about each year. As there's a disconnect from language to neural activity, it stands that if you change the words you use, you change the perceptions in the mind.

If I told you there was an "aroma" coming from another room, you might imagine delicious smells emanating through the air. If I used the same sentence and, instead, used the word "odor," different perceptions would come to mind. The strategy of reframing is to create a different way of observing something. Words have power. That's where we'll start this journey.

My average day is ruled by the calendar as I schedule appointments with clients for hypnotic success coaching. Sometimes life gets in the way. A client's child gets sick and needs to be picked up from school. The cold weather and light rain suddenly became a foot of snow. Charles Tebbetts was a legend in the hypnosis world. He's known for the advice: "Deal with what emerges." Life happens, so we connect by phone or email to reschedule.

There are clearly exceptions to the above. In spite of automated email appointment reminders, someone just forgets to show up. It's around 2pm, and someone calls to tell me they're too busy at work to make their 4pm session. Their business is important to them, but, then again, so is mine. Given the typical waiting period for a new client to see me, the time is lost when someone else could have made use of the time. While things are going well in the financial state of my business, the loss of time equates to some loss of income.

Many businesses protect their time with a cancelation fee. Realize that the words, "cancelation fee" convey a very negative message. These words may suggest that "You wasted my time, and now you have to pay for it as a punishment." This is not the tone I choose to use when communicating with my clients. Maintain the integrity and respect of your business, but mix in some of the golden rules. You might be surprised to learn I dropped the "cancelation fee" from my business. The relationship with my clients dramatically improved as a result of this. However, if they cancel without notice, they still pay for the time.

"But wait a minute, you said you got rid of your cancelation fee!" I hear some of you cry.

I did. It just evolved into something else. It became a "rescheduling policy." This is, admittedly, a rare issue in the way I run my business, but for the times it becomes an issue, people readily pay the fee and reschedule.

Analyze the words for a moment. "Cancelation" is a harsh word that suggests something is coming to an end. "Fee" conveys the feeling of a penalty. If you call it that, and enforce it as such, you'll likely damage the relationship you've worked so hard to build.

Alternatively, "rescheduling" suggests we're continuing the process we've built. "Policy" suggests it's something we've already agreed to. This policy is clearly explained in advance, so there isn't a surprise should we need to make use of it in either my hypnosis or business mindset programs.

People call my business asking for "sessions." We end up arranging a "program."

My programs don't have a "cost." Instead, as I introduce the program, they learn the rates as an "investment."

We made use of HypnoBirthing for my wife to give birth to our son without pain relief medication. In that program, the author Marie Mongan reframes terms such as "pain" into "pressure" or the experience of a "contraction" into a "surge." The shift of words changes the perception of the experience.

Use common sense and care when doing this. Reframing a scenario with choice language can be a benefit. It can also become ridiculous. I once had a maintenance issue at an office I rented that the engineers branded as "structural interruption," "water intrusion," and "organic growth." Call it what it is. The foundation was cracked, my walls and carpet were drenched, there was black mold growing behind the walls, and I quickly moved my business out of that space.

Reframing goes beyond words. Think about a goal you haven't yet achieved. Have you been holding onto a story as to why it's not the right time? What if you decided every current conflict was the best reason to make the goal happen even faster?

Apply this concept to your own emotions. Two people are about to walk onto a stage and deliver a presentation. One of them reports that they feel "terrified" to step in front of the audience. The other feels "excited." They both might be feeling the same physiological sensations. One labels them as fear, while the other puts these feelings to use.

It only took a few moments for an executive I coached to rapidly change her thinking about her health. She used to emotionally eat in response to stress. She soon decided that "Everything is energy. If I'm feeling stress, there's heightened energy in my body. Food is measured in calories. Calories are just a measurement of energy. If there's increased energy in my body, I don't need to add more energy. If I'm feeling more energy, I need to burn away the excess energy." The mental change occurred in seconds. The emotional eating was gone. She lost the desired weight in a few, short weeks. As an unexpected benefit, she also found her best problem-solving happened as she went for regular walks.

Reframing can be expanded to large organizations. I delivered my corporate keynote to an insurance group that was losing productivity. Their staff had been operating in fear of layoffs, as this was becoming a standard in the industry. The pattern at other organizations was that they were firing full-time employees only to then attempt to rehire the same people as independent contractors based on commission. They feared they'd lose the promise of a steady income and benefit package. These horror stories were playing out across the industry, though not yet within this specific group.

I met with their executive team for my presentation's needs analysis. As it often does, our conversation shifted to the bigger picture of the event. They renamed a new employee benefit program a "family benefit." They stopped using the language of "employees" to instead call their team "partners" or "members." At the banquet where my keynote would be the feature, the executive team abandoned the idea of having the management sit on an elevated dais. They instead sat at the tables with their staff. In addition to the feedback I received from my presentation, I still remember someone commenting how nice it was that the CEO stood in line at the buffet with everyone else.

Reframing makes it easy to show rather than tell. Observe a challenge from another angle. Make the roadblocks in your story the starting point of a new one.

Exercise creativity as you put this to use.

WORK SMART ACTION STEPS:

☞ Are there negative words you've discovered that have become a frequent theme in your life? Write them down. Brainstorm alternatives. This begins as a conscious exercise to remember to label things differently. It may soon become a massive unconscious shift, setting change into motion.

☞ Explore the idea that an environmental change may be helpful to you. I coached a work-from-home website designer. She achieved better productivity when she traded her pajamas and sofa for a business suit and desk, even though she launched this business to work from home. The result? She really felt like she was "going to work" and her productivity exploded. Are there changes you can make to your environment?

CREATE RAVING FANS

Driving my car into a mailbox taught me everything I needed to know about asking for client testimonials. We've already discussed how positive feedback from your past clients is an incredible asset that can be leveraged into future business. When people discover your product or service, it's as if their automatic reaction is to ask, "Yeah, but does it work?"

I'm going to walk you through the exact method I've used for years to get feedback from my clients. I've used the model across different platforms, whether it's product sales or speaking, though I'll detail it specifically as it would play out in my office. I tell my private clients that my model of business is "raving fans" rather than "lifelong dependents." Build a community that supports your work and promotes it without having to be asked. As people have a great experience with you, they will be happy to tell their story. This builds a solid foundation for a successful, thriving business.

We live in an era of social proof. All media is social. Whether it's online communities, video sites, or even local news, everything is now social. Allow me to paint a glamorous image for you. I'm writing this chapter in a New Jersey hotel prior to a speaking engagement. How did I pick this place to stay the night? Online reviews. Price, convenience, and location were obvious factors in the decision. The positive reviews online let me know I was going to be in good hands here. One review cautioned me about the quality of the continental breakfast. This warning proved to be valid. I enjoyed the travel luxury of two protein bars from my travel bag. The customer feedback momentum will continue after I check out. I'll leave a positive review online, perhaps making suggestions about how to improve the breakfast.

Do you look at reviews when shopping online? Social proof gives you a feeling of safety and security. In hypnosis terms, it lets you mirror someone else's story and walk through their journey. As their story aligns with yours, you're more likely to make the buying decision.

Shift your thinking to the testimonial's hidden benefit. It improves the experience of the person giving it! Yes, though the client feedback experience benefits the growth of your business, it also benefits the person who already had the positive experience. It's validating the improvement they've made. It affirms that they made the right decision.

But what about driving my car into a mailbox? On a cold, winter morning, I was driving very slowly, with extreme caution, in my neighborhood. Even though I carefully turned the steering wheel to go home, my car followed the momentum and kept sliding with no change of direction. My vehicle impressively knocked over the neighborhood's centralized mailboxes. The exterior of the car was heavily damaged. Time for an insurance claim!

The work was soon completed at a local body shop. Their customer service was outstanding and their communication inspiring. "The work is complete. Your insurance covered everything. However, I'm sorry to inform you that you'll need to wait an extra fifteen minutes because we took the liberty of repairing several other minor scratches on your car. The shop is almost done with a complimentary detailing of your car. Do you mind filling out a brief survey while you wait?"

Genius. Talk about under promise, over deliver! Rather than a nameless repair shop suggested by my insurance company, the process of sharing my story drove me to realize how well things went. I now know this business by name, and I've since referred others to them. Raving fans rather than lifelong dependents. I hope to never need this service again, but, if I do, I know where to go. I emerged from the experience a raving fan, and, yes, I'm now more a cautious driver on ice.

Model this experience for your own business. Here's how I've done it. I elicit client feedback once we've successfully completed a presentation or program. If it's a coaching client, I'll ask, "Hey, do you have a few minutes before you head out?" This question establishes two important frames. First, we're about to wrap up. And, second, this will only take a few minutes. I've never had someone respond "No" to this question.

I then say, "I'd like to share with you a quick exit survey to get your feedback on our time together. You probably saw several of these on my website or saw the book with dozens of them in my lobby. Your positive story helps to inspire others. Would you mind filling one out please?"

Take note, this process was suggested in advance. The document they're about to receive isn't something new to them. They've seen these documents before in my promotion. It's one-page, it's quick, and it's an easy form to complete.

They say "Yes," and I reply, "Great. Thanks so much. Feel free to share as much or as little as you like. And if you'd rather I not use your full name in sharing your story, it's fine to just sign the form with your first name."

I now have hundreds of past client survey forms displaying the success of my business.

Take note of how this experience has played out.

First, they've already seen this document on my website or in a book in my office. This is an environmental suggestion that people who work with me complete these surveys. It plants a seed like the jars of cigarettes in my office. The nonsmokers walk into the space ready to throw out their cigarettes. My clients already expect that they'll be completing a survey.

Second, I asked a question that always elicits a yes response. I'm conditioning a "yes" response prior to asking the real question for which I wish to hear a "yes" response.

Third, there's a sprinkle of reframing in this. I never use the word testimonial. It's an "exit survey." If you take just one thing from this "Create Raving Fans" chapter, please let this reframing be it!

Fourth, I offer full transparency as to what will be done with the document with the option to let it remain anonymous.

Now you have an asset! Post it on your website. Share it on your social media streams. Transcribe the written text into an email with the polite request to share their story as an online review. Archive them as specific case studies to share when receiving a unique request.

My current favorite strategy is to go after what I call the "longevity testimonial." It's good to have a positive story about your business. It's amazing when the story begins, "Jason worked with me eight years ago, and I'm still seeing improvements in my life!"

Are you just getting started in business? Instead of taking your full fee or a reduced payment, consider trading your services for a testimonial. I've coached some of my business students to use the phrase, "Assuming our time together goes as well as we both know it will, rather than my full fee, can I count on you to share a feedback survey that I might use in my business promotion?" This strategy has helped several start-up businesses launch with raving fans.

Brainstorm the things you can ask on your survey. My preferred method is fill-in-the-blank sentences for the client to finish.

"We hired Jason because _____."

"The best part of the presentation was _____."

"Our staff's response to the speech was _____."

This also works for video testimonials.

Never stop asking for feedback. I have binders full of these physical documents, yet I keep gathering more of them. These stories will continue to inspire your future clients to work with you while continuing to inspire you to keep growing your business!

WORK SMART ACTION STEPS:

☞ Brainstorm appropriate ways to make getting client feedback a natural part of your process. Too many businesses ask for testimonials in such a way that it's a surprise to their clients. Plant seeds early on that it's a natural part of the experience.

☞ Stay ethical. I met a business owner who would only allow a specific coupon to be used in her business if you left a review for her business online. Even worse, she was requesting the testimonial before the service was complete. Don't do this. It's a nice gesture to provide some extra benefit as a thank-you to those who help you, although I don't endorse the idea that someone can't receive something because they're being forced to leave a review.

☞ Create your own survey. You know the things that people typically say about your business. Consider my fill-in-the-blank idea to make it easier for your client.

Model the survey form we use at Virginia Hypnosis by visiting:

https://JasonLinett.com/wsbsurvey/

PACING AND LEADING

It's time to learn a hypnotic language pattern!

You are about to learn a simple and direct method of positively guiding communication to become more influential. Learn this method, and you'll be able to put it to use right away.

I'll make a disclaimer, however. I'll most often talk about this theme as a branded two-word phrase: "Ethical influence." Almost anybody can sell something once. "Once" is the key. My goal is to help you put a positive message and service out to the world. Build raving fans along the way. If your morals or quality of work are not in alignment, you might crash and burn as you don't deliver on your promises and receive negative reviews.

On the other hand, is your business making a positive impact on the world? Is its value represented in your efforts and the results people achieve? If both of these statements are true, it's your ethical responsibility to use every appropriate technique to inspire more people to join you!

Let's talk about "pacing and leading."

A "pacing" statement is one that shares a sensory, verifiably true statement or feeds back an undeniable fact. The important thing about pacing is to not add a new judgment opinion in the statement. You wouldn't say, "We're having a positive meeting." Instead, you could say, "We're meeting here today."

Here are a few more examples:

Notice the temperature in the room.

Hear the sound of my voice.

Feel the sensation of the chair you're sitting on.

Look at the contract in front of you.

Again, these examples do not carry a judgment or opinion. I'm not saying that it's warm in here or that you enjoy the sound of my voice. I'm making a factual statement to create the momentum of unconscious agreement. To make an opinion invites judgment, which is a conscious mind activity. This breaks the rhythm you're learning to establish.

A judgment may be part of your pacing statement if it's an opinion that has already been expressed. I could say to someone, "We're here to discuss your upcoming convention because last year's event wasn't as successful as you had hoped" if they've already expressed that opinion. Get in sync in conversation by reiterating themes that are already present.

You could simply say, "We're here to discuss your upcoming convention."

Let's move on to "leading."

A leading statement is a suggestion to take an action, shift a belief, or create some other kind of change.

Some examples are:

"You're ready to get started."

"Sign the contract now."

"Discover a new way of looking at this problem."

If I began a meeting by saying to somebody, "You're ready to get started," it would come across as too bold a statement. Blocks would be created in our communication. Consider this alternative phrase:

"We're meeting today because you told me you'd like to grow your business, and you've been looking for a service to help with your search engine results. You've been dealing with the frustration of trying to program it all yourself, and that means, you're ready to get started having someone else do the work for you, right?"

Note the rhythm that is established when the leading statement comes after three pacing statements. The pacing statements are mirroring back previous discussion points. I shared this principle and example with a social media marketing company. They're now converting more prospects into clients. The appropriate sequencing and delivery metaphorically put the foot in the door, so the buyer is ready to take action.

Let the classic cartoon *Schoolhouse Rock* be an inspiration here. "Conjunction junction, what's your function?" The use of the word "and" ties together the pacing statements, establishes a rhythm of communication, and naturally leads into the leading statement.

For extra credit, there was a tag question at the end of the sequence. Simply asking the question "Right?" gets them to go inside their own thoughts, create a brief internal trance, and check in with the statement. It's a mini "Yes Set" to stack the ethical influence and positive buy-in.

Swap the word "and" for the phrase "which means" and you're now building what's called a "Complex Equivalence." You're still pacing and leading; however, you're doing it with more flair.

Here's a recent example from a home contractor:

"You want to look at your attic access because you want to expand your home storage, which means you'd like to review some installation options, right?"

The focus of the sentence is now on the second half of the phrase. You're driving them out of the "no room in my home" problem state into a "get the work done" solution state. Because you read the example, you also realized that demonstrated a complex equivalence. Right?

As you're reading this chapter, perhaps you've already noticed I've been using this linguistic pattern in most of my writing, haven't you?

You can also use previous leading statements as new pacing statements.

As you're understanding how you can use these patterns in your communication, you're realizing there's value in putting these strategies to use.

And as you put these strategies to use, you discover a greater desire to continue learning.

As you realize that value in expanding your education, perhaps you've thought about visiting my websites to learn about my online courses and live training.

It's that easy.

This grows better with practice. As you practice this technique, perhaps scripting a few out for yourself, you'll soon discover a greater confidence in "freestyling" this language pattern conversationally.

As your ethical influence confidence continues to grow, you'll realize there's power in actively listening, which means you're better enabled to resolve conflict or handle typical buying objections.

As your skills grow in becoming more flexible in your communication, you'll realize the power you have to grow your business now.

WORK SMART ACTION STEPS:

☞ The more you listen to people speak, the more you'll likely realize this is based on effective communication. As you adopt this language pattern into your regular speech, you'll likely discover you naturally become more influential.

☞ This doesn't have to be scripted. Though you can have some rehearsed "chunks" ready to go for the common experiences in your business, perhaps. When it comes time to ask for the sale or make a specific offer, you can be ready with this influential communication pattern.

ANCHORING

My daughter is only three months old, and she is deeply asleep. I'm supposed to be out catching up with friends. My wife and I have traveled thousands of miles away for a friend's wedding. She is already in the hotel's lobby with our friends. I'm supposed to put our little girl in the stroller and head down to the lobby, but, again, she's asleep. She's sleeping on me. I'm on the hotel bed on my back, and there's a little face with her eyes closed inches away from my face. There's that half-smile babies are known to make while sleeping.

Time stands still. Nothing else matters.

My phone is within reach, so I text a photo of the situation to my wife. "Have fun, I'm good up here" is all I have to send.

I close my eyes, breathe in fully, and exhale a long, slow, relaxing breath. I want to hold onto the deep connection of peacefulness and my love for my daughter. I want to hold onto this sensory experience.

I focus on her sleeping weight on my chest and the sound of her breathing. With my eyes closed, I repeat the slow, focused breath, taking in the full experience.

Now, more than seven years later, I can close my eyes, breathe that same, focused breath, and fully bring back the kinesthetic experience.

It's more than just the breath. I can feel the muscles in my body melt and stress drain away as I repeat this focused breath.

Behold, the power of anchoring.

The results can be magical, though it isn't magic.

You already know how to do this. You hear a song on the radio. The memories of what you may have experienced as you first heard the song come back to your mind. A smell comes into the environment, triggering the memory of locations or people you've been around before.

Anchoring is the principle of connecting one sensory verifiable experience to another sensory verifiable experience. Our experiences are based on associative memory. This naturally-occurring phenomenon is one you will learn to do on purpose.

Everything is a "state." You have a state of frustration. You have a state of happiness. You have a state of hunger. You have a state of satisfaction. There are states of pleasure, success, exhilaration, and learning. Do a search online for research on "state-dependent learning." If students are relaxed as they learn new information, and if they can achieve the same mental state at the time of exams or tests, they're more likely to recall the information.

Some would liken this to Dr. Ivan Pavlov's studies on classical conditioning. He rang a bell every time he fed the dogs in his laboratory, and they wound up salivating every time he rang the bell. What makes this different is the hypnotic ability to tap into the mental and emotional states, not just behaviors.

Donald Hebb, a Canadian psychologist, is credited for the understanding that "neurons that fire together, wire together." This is known as Hebb's rule. As two parts of your mind activate at the same time, they link together creating a new connection.

Anchors should be simple yet specific. The posture of my chest muscles and the deep slow breath is the anchor I can use nearly a decade later to bring back the same mental state of timelessness, love, and relaxation.

A "best practice" tip is to combine two sensory elements for your anchor to be specific. A deep breath and the squeeze of a fist. A shift in visual focus and standing upright. A smile and a clap of the hands. The position of your hands holding the golf club and the posture of your shoulders. Anything can become an anchor. You can train your actions to "Be Hypnotic" in addition to doing a formal process of hypnosis.

Anchors become effective either through repetition or through intensity. When I close a successful sales phone call, I smile and clap my hands once. It's a silly ritual, yet, to be fair, I'm in a room by myself. I close another sale, I repeat the ritual. When the phone is dialing to follow-up on a potential contract, I repeat the ritual. Now I'm "in the zone," receptive to the needs of my client and navigating the sales process. I built this anchor through repetition.

When my daughter was asleep on my chest, it only took once or twice to build the anchor. The positive intensity of the experience was enough fuel to build the connection.

Your environment can also become an anchor. Through a brief bit of self-hypnosis, I'd close my eyes and imagine the threshold of the doorframe on exiting my office. This could act as a cleansing mechanism. I conditioned my mind to expect that passing through the doorframe would release the "business time" mode I was in to have a clean slate for the next part of my day. This mental exercise is how I leave the office with as much energy as when I first walked into the space. This is also a big part of the appropriately compartmentalized world I've built. When it's time to work, it's time to work. When it's not, I'm present to the world around me.

Bring your thoughts to a specific positive memory. If it helps to close your eyes when you do this, that's fine (assuming you're not operating heavy machinery). Relive the experience with your sensory awareness in as much detail as possible. What can you hear? Are you connecting with specific images? What's that feeling in your body? Are there any smells coming to mind?

You're about to learn what I call "the anchoring sandwich." Between two moments of increasing the state of mind you're generating, you'll establish the anchor. Turn it up. Build the anchor. Turn it up even more.

Go into that positive mental experience with as much sensory awareness as you can create. There's no right or wrong. However you experience this is what's right for you.

When you feel you have it near the peak, create a specific anchor. The specificity is easy as long as you choose two sensory actions. A breath and a fist. The squeezing and pulsating of a finger and thumb.

As you hold onto that positive state you've created, establish your anchor, and turn it up even more. This is the sandwich. Turn it up, anchor it, and turn it up even more.

Now break the state. Disconnect the anchor and shift your physiology and focus elsewhere. Look somewhere different. Move your body. Now repeat the entire sequence again.

It's as if you're installing a new software program in your mind. As you're creating it intentionally, the method is to use repetition. Run this sequence several times, then put it to use. Fire off your anchor in the scenarios you choose for it to be effective.

Eventually, the "technique" of this falls away. The more you make use of this method, the better it will work for you. The better it works for you, the less you're going to need it. You've conditioned the new automatic response.

Our brains are hard-wired to establish new neural connections, and the skill of anchoring will empower you to build these connections on purpose.

WORK SMART ACTION STEPS:

☞ What are your natural "in the zone" states? Realize you can copy-and-paste one part of life to another. Take a positive feeling from one part of life, create an anchor for it, and fire it off in another part of life. I once had a lawyer create incredible confidence by taking the feelings he experienced while playing basketball with his friends into his closing arguments. Model your own states of excellence.

☞ You can also "stack" your anchors. Bring several emotional states into one specific gesture, posture, or word to design your own peak performance state of mind.

☞ Receive a self-guided hypnotic audio program to create your own confidence anchor for free by visiting:

https://JasonLinett.com/wsbconfidence/

THE "SERIAL KILLER STRATEGY"

The concept of this strategy begins with a reframe. Take the simple idea of mind-mapping and give it a ridiculous name. Now it's memorable! Mind-mapping is a visual strategy where you draw lines between ideas on paper or in computer software. I've made the process more kinesthetic and flexible, and somehow, the nickname "The Serial Killer Strategy" stuck!

You know the scene in the movie. The detectives have been hunting down a killer, and they finally discover the secret room of their prime suspect. The walls are covered with photos of the victims, news stories about their crimes, and strings connecting all the pieces. I'll admit the content of the example is not inspiring, yet the context of the image was the strategy I needed to map out high-value products, programs, and live events.

An executive client came into my office a few months ago to work on his public speaking strategy. His eyes glanced into my storage room where an entire wall was blanketed with Post-It notes; frantically scribbled phrases written on the bits of sticky paper. I can admit the image had to be alarming.

"Is everything alright?" he asked.

"Absolutely. That's a book I'm writing." And it's the one you're reading now.

The "Serial Killer Strategy" takes brainstorming and turns it into a physical experience. If you work on paper, you create the challenge of erasing and rewriting information as you explore an idea. If you work on a computer, the technology sometimes can hold back the creative experience. Or, perhaps, you get distracted by the million other things your computer can do.

Find an empty wall. Grab a stack of Post-It adhesive notes and a pen. Start to brainstorm whatever your next project is going to be. Is it the content of a training session? The features of a product? In the first phase of this strategy, just create the pieces and stick them to the wall. Don't worry about where they go. Just put them up there.

If a wall isn't available, purchase a big sheet of posterboard. The added benefit is now your project is mobile. The book currently in your hands was mapped on half-sized posterboard sheets, which I carried back and forth from my home to the office in an artists' portfolio case.

When you have enough pieces, start to move them around. Is your product or service going to a singular thing or perhaps a modular experience? Will you create a linear course or a choose-your-own-adventure method of learning? As you look at all the sticky papers on the wall, the delivery mechanism of the program may explain itself. Additional ideas may also pop up, so the fact that you can re-stick the papers to the surface makes it more flexible.

Remember the story of the actor turning his back on the audience so he could make another entrance? When you feel you've got the project just right, walk away from it. Give it a few hours. Wait a day or two. Then go back to it and explore the workflow again.

Only after you've got the idea mapped out, grab a sheet of paper or computer and convert your mind-mapped concepts into an outline. Now, you're ready to begin creating.

WORK SMART ACTION STEPS:

☞ It's arts-and-crafts time! Hit your local office supply store and invest in some Post-It notes. Find space on a wall or perhaps use the mobile posterboard solution. Don't get caught up trying to make sure the materials are "just right." This strategy is supposed to be the messy part of planning your project. With full respect to the 3M corporation, spend the money on name-brand Post-It notes. Theirs really are the best.

☞ Consider one of your entrepreneurial concepts and translate it into this physical mind-map project. Have the user experience in mind as you realize breaking a massive concept down into smaller chunks makes the customer's journey more comfortable. It makes your design process even easier.

GET THE RESULT BEFORE YOU GO FOR THE RESULT

You've likely heard that some people in business stand in the way of their own success because they are too cautious to ask for the sale. What if there was a way to open up your full sensory perception to calibrate when your potential buyer is already sold on your process? Imagine the growth of your business when you tap into the ability to only ask for the sale when you know you've already made it?

This may sound like you're going to learn some kind of hypnotic, Jedi mind-trick. In some ways, yes, yes you are. What you're really about to learn is a method to appropriately stack value, so your buyer is primed to make a decision that's already a done deal. The obvious disclaimer, once again, must be repeated. Please only use your powers for good.

Think about the person who signs up to run a half-marathon. They spend several months training, gradually increasing their endurance to run long distances. By the time race day arrives, there isn't much doubt as to whether or not they'll finish. It's going to happen, it's just a matter of how long they'll take.

Consider: a family decides to move their home. The offer is accepted, the contract has been ratified, and it's now a game of waiting until the closing date. The last inspection of the property goes well. They've even paid down some debt in advance of the final mortgage review. There's little doubt the contracts will be signed and the keys handed over. It's a done deal.

Remember the lesson on relationships from "Harness Lead Generation?" I didn't approach the girl at college who would become my future wife and say, "We're going to have children." The telling of this story earlier in this book would cause you to assume I first asked her out on a date. That's not the entire story. I left out a very important detail. Allow me to rewind the story back a little further. We met working together on a student project, and we did not get along. It wasn't like we were fighting or yelling, it's more like we just got on each other's nerves. The project was completed, and, in spite of our rocky work relationship, we still hung out with each other. I knew I liked her, yet I hesitated to move things forward.

I didn't first ask her out. Instead, I asked her permission if it would be okay if one day I could ask her out. You read that right. I believe the clinical term of this situation would be that I was "chicken." If she said "No" to my asking permission to could ask her out, it wasn't like she had said no to my asking her out, because technically, I wasn't asking her out, right? She didn't say "No." She said "Yes." It took me at least two weeks to eventually work up the real courage to ask for the date. Thanks to my "market testing," I already had the answer. She said yes, and now we've been together for more than fifteen years.

There's a correlation between the marathon runner, the family buying the home, and my cautious beginning to an amazing relationship. We got the result before we asked for the result.

I've applied this principle in my work as a hypnotist. Whether I'm speaking to a group of business people or working privately in my office, there's often a moment by way of hypnotic suggestion where a person's arm becomes stiff and rigid as a steel bar. The more they try to bend it, the stronger it feels. In my delivery of this, the subject often has their eyes open, and they're laughing at how unique the experience feels. They know it's the same arm they've carried around their entire life, yet, in this moment, it won't bend! The benefit of this experience is that it helps a person validate the experience of hypnosis, rather than just feeling the experience of deep relaxation. It eliminates the virus in the hypnotic profession of someone saying, "I felt relaxed, but I don't know if I was hypnotized."

Many practitioners don't use this method due to fear it might not work. Rather than say, "That doesn't work," my intention is always to ask, "How do I make it work better?"

I previously mentioned the idea of stacking value. So, by the time you make the sales offer, it's virtually a guaranteed "yes" response. I apply this concept to this moment. I stack a number of hypnotic principles to fully compound the intended result that it's as if the arm won't bend. I put my complete focus on the person's arm, so I can observe the moment the "magic" effect kicks in. My language includes the patterns of "Feel your arm getting stronger and stronger, stiff and rigid like a steel bar!" My language patterns pivot to "Try to bend that thing, and it gets stronger and stronger!" once I see the hypnotic effect has already taken place.

I only go for the "testing phase" when I'm 100% convinced it's already been achieved. The tone of my voice brings about my laughter and theirs as they enjoy the brief novelty of the situation. And before you can ask, yes, we release the tension so their arm can relax. The hypnotic moment serves as a metaphor for letting go of previous issues that seemed more difficult than they actually were.

Get the result before you go for the result.

Let's now talk business. What if you only asked for the sale when you knew you already had it? What if you asked somebody to take a step forward in a funnel sequence only when you knew they were ready to do so?

When I'm speaking to a group of business people, my primary goal is to deliver the intended message of motivation and personal success. I may also have the goal of people extending this relationship into another speaking engagement, becoming a coaching client, or, perhaps, attending one of my courses. In addition to these goals including financial gains, there's incredible power in having a "list" of people interested in what you do. If it's appropriate for the event, I'll invite people to sign up to receive the regular updates and resources I share by email.

But remember, "Nobody wants your newsletter."

The method I'm about to reveal is what I've found to be the most effective way to motivate people to take action and join my list. Note that I'm not going to pass around a clipboard with the request to "sign up for my newsletter." I'm going to make a specific offer, with the right timing, that will get the maximum result. It takes a little preparation and advance thinking, but here's how it often plays out.

I'll wait for a moment where I notice people writing down some notes about something I've said. I'll now ask a question to establish a checkpoint. "I can see some of you are frantically trying to write down some of these ideas. Would it be helpful if I shared an outline of this presentation with you?" The audience responds "yes." I've just been given permission to someday ask them out on a date. I acknowledge the positive response, though I don't make the offer yet. Are you noticing a trend here?

I'll perhaps do a demonstration with one person from the audience or maybe something experiential for the entire room. "Wouldn't it be great if you could relax that deeply after work to unwind from the day? I have a program I sell on my website that teaches you a similar method. In less than ten minutes, you can dissolve away stress and feel more focused to move on with your day. It's only thirty-dollars on my website, though as a thank you for having me here today, would it be alright if I shared that with all of you for free?" I receive another "yes." I have my second checkpoint that they'd like to advance our relationship, so now it's time to make the ask.

The key here is to be able to provide something that will enhance their experience from the talk. It's not like I'm making an "upsell" offer. Instead, think of it as an "upgrade." The resource they will receive will help them find a benefit more easily and expand our relationship beyond this initial meeting. Value first.

Now I can make the request. "Great, I'll pass around this iPad. Please share your email address to immediately receive those resources, just please make sure it gets around the entire room. If for some reason you miss it, please see me at my table after this program. I'll make sure you get everything I've promised."

Use your favorite method to collect the contact information. There are many "text to opt-in" services you can find online. I would not recommend the texting option if you're speaking to an international audience. A clipboard will work, though I'd suggest having several of them to go around the room. For a small-to-medium sized group, I like using an app called iCapture, a service which integrates with most of the email automation platforms. Thanks to a little technology, the attendees receive the content immediately in their email. I don't have to go home and transcribe anything. Once programmed, it's all automated. Set it and forget it.

This method should sound familiar to you. You previously read a variation of it in the client feedback example in "Create Raving Fans." The client was ready to complete my exit survey before I officially made the request.

Your goal should be to provide value, give a strong benefit to continue communication, and make it easy to take the next step.

If you're selling, demonstrate efficacy and value, apply your product's benefits to the potential buyer so you know it is going to help them, and only then ask for the sale.

WORK SMART ACTION STEPS:

☞ Consider a sales offer or opt-in offer you'd like to make. Consider the customer's journey that begins with visibility and then ends in profitability. Break the process down to the smallest steps from the beginning to the end of the experience. Examine the process for places you can interject "checkpoints" to ensure the potential buyer is in sync with you.

☞ This strategy should reinforce the wisdom in making sure your lead generation opportunity begins with value. The more market research you do to make sure your opt-in offer is something they need, the more likely your list-building will be successful.

☞ If you're single and there's someone you'd like to get to know better romantically, ask them if it'd be okay if you asked them out one day. Hey, it worked for me!

CONSCIOUS REINFORCEMENT

What if the methods of effective advertisements and best-selling music could be your secret for success? You're about to learn one of the simplest and most direct methods I share with people to rapidly refocus the mind to achieve a goal. This is a method to put positive hypnotic suggestions or affirmations on autopilot. The more you read this chapter, the more you're going to realize this strategy has already worked on you. So use it!

"Write down your goals." This is advice I'm sure you've heard hundreds of times. Have you actually done it?

Pause this chapter for a moment to actually do it. Really. Do it right now. It shouldn't take more than a few minutes. For now, focus on only two or three things. Allow it to be the first draft. Back in my management days, I would sometimes employ the strategy of labeling a document "Version 1.2." This implied to the reader and me that it was capable and likely to change. You're allowed to edit this document later.

Remember the pacing and leading strategy? Use this format to put an action to your result.

"As I schedule time for personal development, my ability to grow my business increases."

"By attending more networking meetings, I grow my personal network to fill my office schedule."

"As I review my progress every other month, I set new goals to level up my success."

"Asking my clients for referrals helps me to scale my business year-after-year."

Write down your goals, and you're activating the primary learning abilities of the mind: auditory, visual, and kinesthetic. As you write down your goals, you can feel it. As you look at them, you can see them. As you read them to yourself, even if only in the privacy of your own mind, you can hear them. Rev up your conscious/unconscious engine to take action and set these goals in motion by writing down your goals.

Let's take it one step further. Open up some recording software on your computer, or, even better, the Voice Memo app on your phone. Read your goals over and over into a brief audio file perhaps five to ten minutes in length. You're creating an audio loop that you're going to use for "Conscious Reinforcement."

If you want to get low-tech in a high-tech way, consider burning a CD of the voice track. Compact discs. Remember those? We were so young. There's a funny reason I suggest this. A friend of mine is an incredible storyteller. He released an album of his stories back in 2013, and, as a gift when we first met, he gave me a copy of his CD. Almost six years later, that's the same CD still in the player in my car. Physical media is now a relic from the past, as I'm likely to stream music in my car from my phone. Burn a CD of your goals, and they'll always be in your car.

If any of the above recommendations are beyond your technical skill, ask a teenager for help.

Now, as you're commuting in your car, have the goals playing in the background. You don't need to give it your full conscious awareness. Let it become repetition in the background. Play it in your home as you're taking care of simple tasks like getting ready in the morning or cleaning. Whatever scenario you choose, the strategy is to have the voice recording playing in the background for a minimum of ten minutes a day.

It's low effort for maximum reinforcement. As you do this, you'll be achieving the same psychological benefit that advertisers and recording artists have known for years.

Think about it. You've never turned on the television with the goal of memorizing the slogans of popular products. Which breakfast cereal is magically delicious, and which one snaps, crackles, and pops? Do you know the energy drink that gives you wings? What makeup product asks you "Maybe she's born with it?" Which shoe manufacturer encourages you to "Just do it?" If you had to buy batteries, would you be drawn to the one that just "Keeps going, and going, and going?" What credit card in your wallet is "Everywhere you want to be?"

I would even bet that you could answer some of those questions, and you've never bought the product!

There are lyrics to songs that you know, and you've never sat down with the intention of studying the words and committing them to memory. You know all the words.

"So no one told you life was gonna be this way?"

(Clap clap clap clap)

You've never intentionally focused on these lyrics or advertising campaigns, yet those messages are stuck in your brain. You don't have to listen, you pick it up unconsciously.

As advanced as our minds are, they're a little more low-tech than we'd like them to be. For my video projects, I had to format a four-terabyte hard drive the other day for additional storage. In less than 10 seconds, the drive was wiped clean. The brain doesn't work that way. Think of it more like a VHS cassette tape. You couldn't just click a button and delete a two-hour recording on a videotape. You'd have to record over the old programming.

This "conscious reinforcement" strategy helps you do that. It helps you to overwrite patterns of negative self-talk.

"Nothing works for me."

"I'm going to have a miserable time at that event."

"People don't appreciate my work."

Write down your goals, put action to them, record them, and put them on a loop in your life. If it works so well for advertisers, make it work so well for you. Change the inner dialogue now to what you want, rather than what you don't want.

WORK SMART ACTION STEPS:

☞ Create several goals using the action/result formula. Write them down to lock in the auditory, visual, and kinesthetic learning.

☞ Use whatever level of technical skill you're comfortable with to record at least a five-minute loop of you saying those goals in an affirmative tone. The easiest solution is to a use a Voice Memo app on your phone.

☞ Play it on repeat in the background frequently throughout your day. This is a hypnotic process that doesn't require a deep state of hypnosis or eye closure, so you can do it practically anytime and anywhere.

SELF-HYPNOSIS

You're about to learn a self-hypnosis method I've shared with thousands of people. It only takes a few minutes, and you don't need any "props." Even better, it begins with a brief moment of hypnotic phenomenon you can safely create for yourself. I've received great feedback on this method from the audiences I've shared it with, and I'm excited for you to put it to use.

Many people ask me what's the difference between hypnosis and meditation. These are both what can be called "category" words. There are many forms of hypnosis, and there are various styles of meditation. I'll share a blanket statement to which there are some exceptions: many forms of meditation seek the goal of clearing the mind, and hypnosis is a process of filling the mind with a specific desired outcome.

There's a myth that hypnosis must be a state of deep physical relaxation. Think about the volunteers in a stage hypnosis comedy program. They're deeply hypnotized, yet some are accepting the suggestion to leap to their feet and dance at the cue of a specific song.

The hypnotic process often begins with creating some form of mental phenomenon. This is exactly what you're about to learn how to do for yourself. We'll use this metaphorical "foot in the door" to open your mind, to create personal change, and to shift your business mindset. You can create a state of mind in which you're now more receptive to a new idea, a new experience, or releasing an old unhelpful pattern.

The formula is simple. Create a hypnotic experience; ride that into a positive outcome.

Just like a hammer, I'd encourage you to think of this process as a tool. It's not that it "works" or "doesn't work" for you. The subjective experience of the process may be different from one person to another, which is why I'm going to share with you a simple process of self-hypnosis that I've shared with people around the world with outstanding feedback on the benefits.

In this process, your eyelids will eventually be closed, and your body will be relaxed. This isn't the time to be driving your car or operating a forklift.

Read through this process first rather than trying to follow along. Process it consciously before you attempt to process it with your unconscious mind. There's strength in the simplicity of this method. To give credit where it's due, the opening of the process is inspired by Dave Elman, a pioneer in the hypnotic profession who lived from 1900 to 1967. Dave had a fascinating life that uniquely started as a vaudeville comedian yet led into a career of teaching doctors how to use hypnotism to benefit their medical practice.

Before we get started, think about your hand. There's no need to perform these actions, just think about them for now. If you really wanted to, you could squeeze your hand into a fist so tightly shut that it would seem as if you couldn't squeeze it anymore. You could also relax your hand. You could relax your hand so thoroughly that it would seem as if you couldn't relax it anymore.

Assuming your hand was relaxed, realize this next statement to be true. If you wanted to take that relaxed hand and squeeze it into a fist, you'd first have to make the decision to release the relaxation. You'd have to let go of the relaxation before you could ever apply the tension necessary to make a fist. As long as you hold onto the relaxation in that hand, you make it so relaxed, it's as if it just doesn't want to work...

Now, bring your attention to your eyelids. Close your eyelids and relax the muscles around your eyelids all the way down. Let them become so relaxed that it's as if they just don't want to work. You'd have to release the relaxation to even let them open. As you focus on that relaxation, notice that you can be the one to make them just not work. Try, and they just relax even deeper.

Quit testing and send that relaxation down throughout your body. Send it down to your feet as if you could imagine all the relaxation that's possible in your body collecting into your feet. Let those feet become so heavy with relaxation that even if you were to try to pick them up, they could just feel even heavier now. Not because I tell you so, but instead, because it becomes your idea and reality that you can make that happen.

Enjoy these changing sensations in your body as you let your imagination take you into your desired outcome. Mentally associate yourself into your desired experience. Instead of watching it like a movie, go inside the experience with as many of your senses as possible. See it as if through your own eyes. Hear the sounds around you. Feel these sensations in your own body. There's no "right" or "wrong" way to do this, however you experience this moment is what's right for you.

Connect with this future result as if you're already there. Mentally rehearse your own success. Become aware of those things you will have done to create this desired result. Try on this new outcome. Notice how well it "fits."

Allow yourself to experience this change so normally, so naturally, so easily, as if this is how it's always been.

When you're ready to associate into this new direction of life, with this outcome as your reality, open your eyelids, and notice how good you feel.

It's that simple. Create the brief mental phenomenon as if the eyelids could become so relaxed as if they don't work. Dave Elman called this "the opening wedge." Transfer and compound the same sensation to the feet. Now that we have the mental opening for suggestion, rely on experiences rather than just words. You could mentally repeat the phrase you created from the "Conscious Reinforcement" strategy, though I've received the best feedback from allowing yourself to hypnotically associate into the desired result.

In a one-to-one coaching session, there are dozens of other strategies to more specifically deal with letting go of past events or resolving inner conflict. With a bit of repetition and mental rehearsal, you can begin to condition your mind to a much more positive outcome on your own.

Focus on what you want rather than what you don't want.

WORK SMART ACTION STEPS:

☞ I suggest starting with one specific outcome for this strategy. Use the technique with the same goal to harness the unconscious mind's ability to create a new mental pathway through repetition. Once you have this change in motion, only then experiment with addressing another goal.

☞ If you think you need to schedule time to do this, you're overthinking it. Instead, fold it into your day in moments of transition. Do it before you get out of bed in the morning to start the day on your terms. Do it just before you start the workday. Use the method before enjoying a healthy meal to eat mindfully and with intention. Put it to use before exercise to warm up the mind as well as the body. I often do it when I get home from work to let work be work and let home be home. Use the method before you fall asleep at night. I've received the best feedback from those who used it as a transitional tool to refocus throughout the day.

☞ To get an audio version of this technique to guide you through the experience, please visit:

https://JasonLinett.com/wsbselfhyp/

PLAY

You can have pizza at the Chinese food buffet. There's one last strategy to share with you.

"Play."

Have fun it with all.

Just like the video game mindset that came from the "Build Rituals" principle, realize that while the growth of your business is a serious process, it's a game in which you can have some fun.

The moment you decide it can be fun is when I often see people skyrocket their success. Get creative and realize that the journey ahead isn't always linear. There will be ups, and there will be downs. Like a rollercoaster, savor the suspense as you climb up the track. Enjoy the excitement as it swoops downhill and flies through amazing loops. Use the principles and the strategies in this book to move to the front of the line.

Visit a Chinese food buffet, and you'll notice the classic favorites. Egg rolls. Sesame chicken. Mixed vegetables with those miniature pieces of corn. Perhaps even some sushi. They also cater to the picky eater, as you'll likely find french fries, chicken fingers, and yes, there's often pizza on the buffet.

Is there something wrong with having the pizza at a Chinese buffet? I don't think so. If you want the pizza, have the pizza. If you want the delicious Asian cuisine, go right ahead.

The literal suggestion here is that there's more than one way to build a successful business. I've shared my story with you to have a model of what's worked for me. The methods have also been successful with many of my audiences, clients, and students. It's gone through vigorous testing before I decided to teach it. Put in the appropriate effort, and you can likely do the same in your field.

The virus to overcome is the "either-or" brick wall. Do I use Twitter or Instagram? Do I build a general website or several specific niche websites? Do I use lead generation or just post my products online?

The answer is both. It's an odd phrase, but as much as I write articles, shoot videos, and create opt-in offers to drive the lead generation engine, I live by the phrase that "sometimes you just have to sell it." With all the funnel marketing in place, the product is still on a sales page somewhere to be discovered and purchased.

Some people are ready to make the decision right away. Why make them jump through hoops? Others need to be coached and finessed until the point they organically make the decision. Both are viable customers. Why ignore one of them?

One of my products flatlined the first time I launched it. The initial sales at least recouped my investment. However, I've since sold more than $300,000 of this product. I can count at least two dozen pathways I've created to let people know it exists and share the value.

Design your business to run as several systems operating in place. Just like Ron Popeil and his audience would call out, these systems can become metaphorical machines that allow you to "Set it and forget it."

Build the funnel sequence AND the landing page. Automate the social media content to broadcast on all the appropriate channels. Which is better than the other? You'll never really know until you test your market. I don't know which the best for you is either. I'm a hypnotist, not a psychic.

Testing is the only method to discover the answer. Learn the mechanisms your audience best responds to and that will inform your next strategy. Create multiple pathways that all lead to the same desired result of someone purchasing from you.

Be focused with your efforts, though it's often okay to do a little bit of everything.

Enjoy your pizza.

WORK SMART ACTION STEPS:

☞ As you've read through this book, I hope many of your goals have now become specific action plans. You've had plenty of time to define your intended outcomes. Consider the office-supply-adventure of "The Serial Killer Strategy" to map out all the various ways someone can become your client.

☞ Go for a small win. Rather than getting stuck trying to guess which method of sales will be the best for you, start with the one you know how to do. The results may be slow at first as you continue your market research, but this first system can now begin to run as you build other machines to grow your business.

CONCLUSION

STAY HUMBLE

I have a passion for ongoing education. My car is a mobile university. My daily commute is a time to continue listening to an audiobook or podcast.

As much as I'm on a platform delivering my programs, I'm also frequently attending a workshop as a student to model other people's success. The organizer of a major convention recently called me out on being one of the only paid speakers who paid to attend other people's workshops at the same event.

I revisit information I've previously learned. I'll go through a course to review something I learned years ago to help sharpen my mental tools, learn new methods, or sometimes realize I've needlessly overcomplicated a simple concept.

I attended a workshop years ago to observe a colleague's style of work. We are in the same business, yet it's clear we each have our own individual style. The instructor highlighted me in a friendly way to comment, "Jason does this all the time as he sees a lot of clients. Watch him, he's really good at this."

I embraced the praise like a badge of honor. The instructor was a good friend, a respected person in his profession, and indeed, we were about to practice something I also teach.

What happened next may surprise you.

I got lost in the practice. I got horribly confused. I had to apologize and start the entire exercise all over again.

"What's going on?" I asked myself. I use this method on a daily basis with my coaching clients. I teach it from the platform as I speak to business groups. What am I missing?

By putting 100% of my focus on the praise and perceived expertise, I temporarily shut down my ability to be receptive to new information. I missed the nuances the instructor had shared to practice a variation of a familiar theme.

By metaphorically patting myself on the back, I was covering my ears to continued growth and learning.

Embrace growth. Look for improvement. Yes, it's just as important to acknowledge your accomplishments and celebrate your victories, though let that inspire you to move forward.

In my weightlifting, there's an exercise with a rather unfortunate name. It's called a deadlift. There's an object on the floor in a "dead" position. Your task is to reach down and pick it up. This sounds simple. However, as your strength improves over time, and it's now a barbell loaded with more than twice your bodyweight, it becomes a highly technical maneuver to do safely.

I hired a personal trainer with the request, "Please show me how to do this without hurting myself." He insisted it was best for me to hire him for four months of twice-weekly workouts. I explained I already had a program I wished to follow and only needed assistance to improve this one weightlifting move.

He told me my form was mostly correct and offered a few pointers to improve the mechanics of the move. "Wow, that's much better," I said as I could feel the immediate change. "I can see with practice I'll get better at that."

The look on his face was now one of utter surprise.

"What did you say?" he asked.

A bit confused, I replied, "I can see with practice I'll get better at that."

"Nobody says that to me," he responded. "They just say 'That's hard' or 'I can't do that,'" he continued. "Yeah, you just need the one session. You're good."

Celebrate your success. Some of the biggest shifts in people's lives I observe are when they give themselves permission to acknowledge their strength. There may be weaknesses to overcome, yet with some creative solutions and hypnotic tenacity, they can be leveraged into strengths.

Just like exercise, every day may not result in a personal record. Some days it's phenomenal. Some days it's the same-as-yesterday. Some days will be an absolute challenge. There may be days where you need to stop and re-read your testimonials to remind yourself why you started your own business.

There will also be criticism. The more you put yourself out there to the world around you, the more you open yourself up to other people's opinions. You could shrug it off as "haters gonna hate." Let the discomfort of criticism activate the supercompensation to listen, learn, and take appropriate actions.

To WORK SMART is to work with intention, purpose, and focus. There's a learning curve when you're just starting out, and, sometimes, we need an appropriate smack in the right direction. Some of my best friendships are now with people who called me out on how I could have handled a situation better. This empowers you to personally improve and lead by example in your communities.

Be a trailblazer.

Be a pioneer at what you do.

Earn an incredible income as you make the world a better place.

Be hypnotic.

I look forward to reading your story as you WORK SMART.

YOUR
"CALL TO ACTION"

Thank you for reading WORK SMART BUSINESS!

I really appreciate all of your feedback, and I love hearing what you have to say.

Your input helps to make the next version of this book and future projects even better.

Please share a helpful review on Amazon letting me know what you thought of the book.

Thank you so much!

~ Jason Linett

DEDICATION
and
ACKNOWLEDGMENTS

For Michelle, Claire, and Max for incredible love and support to build a successful business and the joy of stepping away from business.

To my parents for being a spark of inspiration to step away from a job and launch their own business.

To Scott Sandland, Dr. Richard Nongard, Dan Candell, Stephanie Skiba, Richard Clark, Karen Hand, Melissa Tiers, Anthony Galie, Michael Ellner, Dr. Tracy Riley, Howard Cooper, James Hazlerig, Ron Eslinger, Sean Michael Andrews, Igor Ledochowski, Michael Watson, Paul Ramsay, Ines Simpson, Mike Mandel, Chris Thompson, Ken Guzzo, Catherine Hickland, Robert & Linda Otto, Michael DeSchalit, Carm Blacconiere, Nick Ebdon, Nicholas Pallesen, Dr. Will Horton, Richard Cole, Bob Burns, Kevin Cole, Sheila Granger, Alain Nu, Jo-Anne Eadie, Marc Carlin, Laura King, Cheryl & Larry Elman, Gary Albert Hughes, Elsom Eldridge Jr., Tim Horn, Jess Marion,

Shawn & Sarah Carson, Marie Mongan, Roy Hunter, Anthony & Freddy Jacquin, Antonio Perez, Adam Eason, Kelley T. Woods, and many others for fostering an incredible hypnotic community and sharing the message that we can help and inspire others.

To Geoffrey Ronning, Chandler Bolt, Sean Sumner, Ryan Deiss, Perry Belcher, Molly Pittman, Russ Henneberry, Kelly Glover, Dr. Robert Cialdini, Pat Flynn, Ron Popeil, Amy Landino, Tim Ferriss, Michael Gerber, Kevin Pollak, Amy Porterfield, Dr. Ivan Misner, Michael Matthews, Chris Ducker, Frank Kern, Jeff Walker, Lise Cartwright, Kris Calixton, and many others for the foundational business strategies to make it all happen.

Special acknowledgments to the rockstars Korey Samuelson, Sharon Bliss, Rosalyn Williams, and Kenneth Lerman for their recommendations to improve your reading experience.

To everyone who was a part of the launch of this project.

To you for taking a step in a new direction to make something big happen in your life.

The more we're all successful, the more we're all successful.

Made in the USA
Middletown, DE
22 September 2023